HOW TO MAKE
BIG MONEY
AT HOME

HOW TO MAKE
BIG MONEY
AT HOME

Ronald J. Cooke

Eden Press
Montréal

HOW TO MAKE BIG MONEY AT HOME
By Ronald J. Cooke

ISBN: 0-920792-68-5
© 1986 Eden Press

First edition. All rights reserved.
No part of this book may be reproduced, stored in a retrieval system, or transmitted in any form or by any means, electronic, mechanical, photo-copying, recording, or otherwise, without the written permission of the publisher.

Cover design: EDDESIGN
Book design: Lynette Stokes

Printed in Canada at Metropole Litho Inc.
Dépôt légal — troisième trimestre 1986
Bibliothèque nationale du Quebec

Eden Press
4626 St. Catherine Street West
Montreal Quebec
Canada H3Z 1S3

Canadian Cataloguing in Publication Data

Cooke, Ronald J., 1913-
    How to make big money at home

ISBN: 0-920792-68-5

1. Home-based businesses.   2. Small business.
3. Self-employed.   4. Success.   I. Title.

HD8036.C66 1986   658'.041   C86-090181-5

*To Mary Alice Daly
whose valuable assistance made
this book possible*

TABLE OF CONTENTS

INTRODUCTION 1
MY FIRST BUSINESS VENTURE 2
CASE HISTORIES 5
    1 He Turned a Dime into a Fortune 5
    2 The Story of Leila Albala 6
    3 Honest Ed's Bargain House 8
    4 He Turned Twelve Watches into a Fortune 10
    5 It All Started in North Bay 11
    6 It Started With Scones 13
    7 The Holiday Inn Empire 14
    8 It Pays to Be on Time 16
    9 The Dog Food Man 17
RESEARCH AND MARKETING 20
THE LOCAL SURVEY 21
MONEY-MAKING SUGGESTIONS 22
    1 Prints from Europe 23
    2 Church Histories Work Out Well 24
    3 Food Specialists 25
    4 The Mail-Order Business 25
    5 Getting into Broadcasting 30
    6 Want to Import Merchandise? 33
    7 The Real Estate Boom 35
    8 The Kitchen-Table Publisher 38
    9 Becoming a Booklet Publisher 42
    10 The Franchise Business 45
    11 Start Your Own Periodical Without Money 51
    12 Starting a Small Newspaper 54
    13 Starting a Consumer/Hobby Magazine 55
    14 Publicity Can Make Sales for You 56
    15 Your Camera Can Become a Money-Making Machine . 60
    16 The Wealthy Shoemaker 63
    17 Be a Printing Jobber 65
    18 Money in Bookbinding 65
    19 Private Mailbox Service 66
    20 Opening a Convenience Store 66
    21 Be a Garage Sale Manager 67
    22 Book Remainders Can Be Profitable 68

23 Odd Jobs...69
24 Videotaping..70
25 Complete Lawn Service............................71
26 Knitting Machines are Money-Makers......71
27 Hand-Knitting Still in Demand..................72
28 Newsletters are Worthwhile......................73
29 Rent a Section of a Large Store...............74
30 Calligraphy is in Demand.........................75
31 Speciality Catering Comes Alive..............76
32 Tutoring at Home.....................................77
33 Teaching Music..77
34 The Sandwich Wagon...............................78
35 Telephone Soliciting Can Pay...................78
36 Furniture Finishing...................................79
37 Delivery Service.......................................80
38 Service Needs..80
39 Steak and Kidney Pies in Demand...........80
40 Dried Flowers are Popular.......................81
41 Complete Catering Service......................81
42 Teaching English.....................................82
43 I Love to Cook...82
44 Repair Appliances...................................83
45 Home Office Service...............................83
46 "We'll Do Anything"................................84
47 Carpet Cleaning is Big Business..............85
48 Manuscript Typing...................................86
49 The Research Business............................86
50 Janitorial Services In Demand.................86
51 The "800" Phone Numbers and Credit Cards.............87
52 Holding Seminars....................................88
53 Land for Quick Cash Crops.....................89
54 Selling Used Vacuum Cleaners................90
55 New Roads — New Opportunities..........91
SOME BUSINESS FACTS..................................92
   The Value of Being Incorporated..................92
   On Getting a Loan..93
   Discounting Your Invoices.............................93
   Loan Firms Can Be Helpful..........................94
HOW MUCH CAPITAL DO YOU NEED?..........96

WHAT ABOUT A PARTNERSHIP?	97
Be Careful Taking Over Leases	97
Businesses for Sale	97
Buying a Business?	98
DON'T BITE OFF MORE THAN YOU CAN CHEW	99
SETTING UP YOUR OFFICE	99
Keep Office Expenses Down	100
Ways of Cutting Starting Costs	101
Get Out if Losses Mount	102
Becoming an "Instant" Millionaire	102
Going Public	104
Can You Protect Your Idea?	105
THIRTEEN STEPS TO SUCCESS	107
NOTES	111

HOW TO MAKE
BIG MONEY
AT HOME

Introduction

With prices constantly rising, a number of people are looking at part-time business opportunities with a view to increasing their income. If you are unemployed, the idea of starting a little business is very inviting, especially if only a minimum amount of capital is required.

Starting a small business with little capital, often in spare hours, is what this book is all about. I have been working for myself for over thirty-five years. My speciality is a combination of writing and publishing. During this period I have interviewed hundreds of business people both in Canada and the United States. Some of the people were with large firms, others I talked to were one-person businesses, often operated from home.

There are many examples of small business ideas on these pages. You'll be surprised at how much you'll learn as you proceed, and you'll find that this book answers many questions.

When it comes to starting a business, it seems that age, sex, or business experience are not all that important. Most successful people have four things going for them; they are enthusiastic, quick-minded, energetic, and are not afraid to *work*. "Work" is the key word, if an idea doesn't succeed, it may simply be that you didn't work hard enough. Many good ideas hit us in the early morning, when the rest of the world is just thinking of getting up. But the important thing is to start; and right now is the best time of all!

Ronald J. Cooke

My First Business Venture

I was nineteen and it was during the depression, I had taken over a small gas station, I needed money. Someone suggested I get a loan from the local bank.

I had two accounts there; one was personal and one was for business. My personal total was seldom more than five dollars. I tried to keep it at least at that figure because the bank paid interest on accounts of five dollars or more. This was three and a half percent annually, and a book I had read on finance stressed the importance of interest. I learned that if you had enough money invested, you could actually live off the interest without working. I intended one day to figure out how much I would have to invest to live off the interest. But right then I was too busy getting the little gas station going that I had recently rented.

I kept my second bank account under the heading of "business." Every day I faithfully made a deposit. I'd put a sign on the door of the station — back in ten minutes — and then I'd run to the bank. I remembered reading a line that had impressed me; it was Ben Franklin, I think, who said, "Look after thy shop, and it will look after you."

My daily business deposit wasn't always big. Sometimes it was only seven or eight dollars. But at other times, when two or three people wanted their tanks filled, my deposit might be as much as fifteen dollars. But in those depression years people usually ordered a maximum of four gallons, which cost them a dollar or less.

At this particular time I needed fifty dollars desperately. My month's rent on the station was due in two days. That wouldn't have been too bad, except that I still owed the previous month's rent. The rent was twenty-five dollars a month. I thought I would borrow sixty dollars, pay the two month's rent, and still have ten dollars left over for emergencies.

For my rent I got a small shack on a corner lot that was about a hundred feet square. Imperial Oil had installed two gas pumps. You had to work your arm off to keep the big glass globes at the top of the pump filled with gas after a sale. Customers liked to see the gas running from the globe, down the long hose, and into their car tank. After all, they wanted to make sure they were getting their money's worth.

But now I was at the bank on Main Street to see the manager, Mr. Sharp. I wondered if that was his real name, or whether the bank had a list of names they tagged on managers to help give customers an idea of the type of person they were dealing with. Was there a Mr. Hard or a Mr. Tuff?

A young woman came up to me and said, "Mr. Sharp will see you now. Go through this door." The door was very heavy and I wondered how elderly ladies could open it. But then I guessed that they didn't have much need for business loans.

I got the door open and spied Mr. Sharp sitting at a big desk in the corner of the room. There were chairs against the walls. No doubt some very important bank business was discussed here. Mr. Sharp was examining some papers . He looked up and pointed to a chair on the other side of his desk. The curtain on his window was drawn back and I could feel the hot sun on my face. It also made it difficult to see. In fact, I thought I may have been squinting. I had read in a business book that people who are expected to grant favours often locate their desk so a strong shaft of light shines on their customers. I think the part I read was called "mentally overcoming your client with strong light." I was glad that I had read it. Maybe he'd read the book too.

Mr. Sharp had a red, florid face, and a bottom row of large white teeth that showed when he smiled. My mother had warned me never to trust a man who shows his bottom teeth when he smiles. However it didn't matter, because Mr. Sharp seldom smiled.

He glanced at me. "You're Mr.?" "Cooke," I said. "I have two accounts with your bank." I wondered if three would have helped any. I guessed not, as the total balance wouldn't have been any larger. "I would like to get a loan," I said. Then Mr. Sharp smiled. "Of course."

A young woman came in and put some papers on the desk. She left quietly and Mr. Sharp looked around slowly, as if to make sure that the door was closed tightly. I looked around too. This was apparently important business. He then asked me various questions, such as where I lived and if I were married. I told him I didn't even have a girlfriend, to which he merely grunted.

He kept making notes, and then he asked me how much I wanted and what it was for. I explained that sixty dollars would be fine. He looked at his papers and said, "I see no problem with that." I began to feel good. I could pay that crusty, miserable landlord who had already had three gas station tenants go under.

Mr. Sharp opened his desk drawer. I thought he must keep the loan money there and that I was going to get my sixty dollars right away. That was convenient. Instead he brought out a piece of paper. "Yes," he continued, "I see no problem. Of course you have some stocks or bonds?" "What?" I asked. "You know," said Mr. Sharp testily, "for collateral." "I don't think so," I said quietly, as if trying to remember. "Well then," continued the manager, "maybe a cosigner, a guarantor?" I stood up. "I'm afraid not."

I was on my way to the door when the young woman opened it and led me to the street door. "Don't take it too personally," she said quietly. "It happens all the time."

Since then I've learned a lot about banks and borrowing money.

Case Histories

It's always fascinating to read how small business people built empires, even though they started with little or no money. Sometimes, by reading how they did it, we can pick up invaluable bits of information. Here are several case histories that I hope will help and inspire you.

1
He Turned a Dime into a Fortune

The year was 1879. Frank Winfield Woolworth was twenty-eight and lived in Lancaster, Pennsylvania. He had tried various things without much success, and decided it was time he did something with his life. One thing he knew for certain was that he wanted to be his own boss. Retailing seemed to be the big thing. Store prices were low in those days, but so were wages. A loaf of bread cost a nickel or less, and a quart of milk about the same. The average hourly wage was ten cents. Kids got a nickel for mowing a lawn, and newspapers cost a penny.

This ambitious young man believed that if he could come up with an unusual idea, it just might work. Then he thought of opening a small store that would have everything displayed in full view for the customer; all items would sell for a nickel or dime. Nothing would be over ten cents. People thought it sounded crazy because there were general stores all over the place selling what he intended to offer — cooking items, sewing needs, jewellery, stationery, clothing items, souvenirs, hair grooming needs, and so forth.

F.W. Woolworth realized that having an idea and being enthusiastic about it wasn't enough. You had to start working at it. He managed to save some money from a small job he had, and he raised more money in other ways — usually by borrowing it — until he had almost one thousand dollars! This was a lot of money in those days. Woolworth then rented a small store and spent four hundred and fifty-nine dollars on goods he thought people would like. He put up a red and white sign with the words "F.W. Woolworth 5¢ & 10¢ Store."

As he gradually got ready for the grand opening, people began to get impatient. They wanted to know what this new store was all about. At last they flocked in. Records show that on that first day, sales amounted to one hundred and twenty-seven dollars and sixty-five cents. Frank Woolworth was overjoyed.

From the first, business was good. His open displays and five and dime idea caught on and he was soon opening stores and appointing managers across Pennsylvania, and then around the country. Today there are five thousand two hundred and seventy-eight stores worldwide; this includes Woolco. The company also owns Richmond Brothers and Kinney Shoes. Sales today run into billions of dollars a year, and the company employs ninety-seven thousand people. Some stores franchise certain departments, such as gifts and souvenirs.

In the past — just as today — it's the good idea that's important. And there are still plenty to be tried!

2
The Story of Leila Albala

Leila Albala is forty-one, married, has two children, and lives in Chambly, Quebec. She was born in Finland, where she lived until she moved to Canada about a dozen years ago. She is an active woman, and through meeting people she soon improved the English she had learned in school back in Finland. She had two skills, neither of which she had promoted to any extent. She had done a lot of sewing for the family and she was an artist.

One day she took her baby daughter to the supermarket. The baby was wearing a dress and bonnet that Leila had made. People were soon asking her where she had bought such beautiful clothes, and where they could get them. When she explained that she had designed the bonnet and dress herself, a number of women asked her if she would make some for their children. She refused, saying that she was too busy.

Next she was asked if she would be able to supply patterns. She had never drawn any patterns, but the requests sounded reasonable, so she agreed. It was not long before someone suggested she produce a book of patterns for baby clothes. "Why not?" she thought. She found that she was able to do all the necessary writing without difficulty and she soon sketched dozens of patterns. Her next step was to find a printer, because the publishers she had contacted showed little interest.

The printer produced five thousand copies of her paperback — a quantity necessary to keep individual prices low. Although publishing was new to her, she was often told later that her one hundred and twenty-two page book looked very professional.

She set the book's price at six dollars a copy, including postage. At this point she really hadn't thought much about marketing it. She occasionally bought magazines at the corner store, and these often contained information about dressmaking. One such periodical was *Family Circle*, an American women's magazine with a seven million plus circulation.

Leila thought they might be interested in her patterns, and she mailed them a copy of her book, a couple of photos of completed patterns, and a short history of what she had been doing. "I was most surprised to see a double-spread (two pages) in an early issue telling about my work and giving my address," she said.

That was about four years ago. Leila says that a few days after the piece appeared, the mail orders started to pour in — more than twenty thousand of them. At one point it took her three days to open the letters, which were stuffed with cheques, money orders, and cash, from people all wanting to buy her book.

She turned her basement into an office, sent out more copies of her book, and got more publicity — pages of it! A few of those doing stories were *National Home Business Report*, *Vogue Patterns*, *Houston Press*, *Chicago Sun Times*, *Calgary Herald*, *Edmonton Journal*, *Montreal Gazette*, *Regina Leader-Post*, *Toronto Star*, and *Vancouver Sun-Province*.

"They all did a great PR job," says Leila, who now talks like an old-time publicity person. In fact, publicity people grind their teeth when they see what a fantastic job she's done. She has now published four books (which have all been well publicized) and has at least four more in progress. Her first four, *Easy Sewing for Infants*, *Easy Sewing for Children*, *Easy Sewing for Adults*, and *Easy Halloween Costumes for Children*, have sold over forty thousand copies. She admits that, as costs went up, she had to raise her prices, but she still works at home, doing most of the work herself except for the occasional bit of spare-time help. Another idea that paid off!

3
Honest Ed's Bargain House

Edwin Mirvish was born into the grocery business. By the time he was fifteen he was going to a Toronto, Ontario, technical school by day and spending his evenings delivering grocery orders to his father's customers. Ed was a boy who asked a lot of questions. One of them was, "Is there any sense in delivering items such as soft drinks or a loaf of bread at all hours when the profit might be a dime or less?"

While he was still in his teens his father passed away and young Ed was suddenly in the grocery business. This was back in 1930, just about the beginning of the Depression, which lasted almost ten years.

Then an idea came to Ed; big volume and low mark-up! His idea was to have a store that offered no frills, no delivery, and low, low prices. Before long he was offering big lost-leaders, to bring people into his Bloor Street store, which he now called Honest Ed's Bargain House. As time went on the store became more and more colourful with flashing neon lights. Some people called it "the circus." Everyone knew where the store was, and knew about the bargain prices. In addition to food, he added hardware, electrical appliances, clothing, footwear, and cosmetics. But it seemed that the food specials were the big crowd pullers. If other stores were charging fifty cents for a dozen eggs, Ed charged fifteen. His argument was that if they came for eggs they might buy a radio. But they'd have to get it home, and no credit was extended. He soon had fifteen checkouts.

Were his merchandising methods right? You better believe it! In addition to the building where he was originally located, he bought the three adjoining buildings and turned the upstairs flats into retail areas. Just recently he added forty thousand additional square feet of floor space. Apparently people believed Ed was like the name of his store — really honest — because he soon had a retail staff of one thousand people in his various businesses. "Give the folks a lot of bargains," he said, "and they'll travel miles to deal with you!"

Although Ed Mirvish hadn't worked for any big chain, he was an expert in merchandising. He decided to smarten up a section of seedy buildings on Markham Street near his store. If people were coming to his store, he reasoned, then they'd shop in the nearby sections too. He brightened and spruced up this decaying avenue. People would visit the store and also explore Mirvish Village, as he called it. It looked like a street in old England, with dozens of boutiques, an old-fashioned ice-cream parlour, and studios for one hundred and fifty artists and potters.

Over the years he acquired a taste for good music and plays. When he heard that the century-old Royal Alexandra Theatre was to be torn down to make room for a parking lot, he bought the building and restored it to its former glory. It was said that the price tag was one million dollars. That was back in the mid-sixties and Ed says that now there are more than fifty-two thousand subscribers, enabling him to bring in top stars of stage and film to perform in the theatre.

The theatre is located in the midst of a conglomeration of old warehouses on King Street West. He bought some of these old warehouses and turned them into show-place restaurants, where everything was really "posh" except the prices. He now has five restaurants, most have three floors and contain many priceless antiques. Some are near the theatre. They specialize in ethnic and Canadian food. The most famous are Ed's Warehouse, Old Ed's, Ed's Seafood, Ed's Italian, and Ed's Chinese. These five restaurants can seat two thousand five hundred people at one time. Sometimes Ed will offer a special deal where patrons can have a meal at one of his restaurants and also see a play for one price.

He recently purchased the Old Vic Playhouse in London, England, and restored it to its former splendour. So far there is no indication of any cluster operations here, but with Ed Mirvish you never know! He's only seventy-two.

4
He Turned Twelve Watches into a Fortune

When Richard W. Sears was twenty-three, he was working as an agent in a small railway station in North Redwood, Minnesota. The year was 1886 and the month was June. It was to be the most memorable month in Richard Sears' life, but on that particular day he had no idea of the changes to come, nor any plans to get into merchandising. He was pondering upon a dozen gold-plated pocket watches sitting in boxes in front of him. The watches had been ordered by a jeweller up the street. Young Sears had dutifully taken the package to the jeweller, who had refused to pay the eighteen dollars C.O.D., saying that he had ordered the watches two months earlier and that they had arrived too late. Richard Sears thought of all the paper work he would have to do if he returned the watches, so he decided to pay the costs himself. This wasn't easy on the salary he made.

He figured out a retail price that would give him a two dollar profit on every watch he sold. That would be better than a day's pay. So he let it be known in railway circles that he had some good timepieces available, and in almost no time he had not only sold out but had to order more.

Within a year he was selling watches by mail, and when people asked for jewellery service, he hired a jeweller to look after this work. He was Richard Sears' first employee. His name was Alvah C. Roebuck. That was the beginning of Sears and Roebuck.

Richard Sears didn't realize he was going to become a merchandising giant, but before long he had produced a small catalogue showing his line of watches.

The Five Hundred and Seventy Page Catalogue

Five years later they produced their first five hundred and seventy page catalogue, filled with all kinds of merchandise. It soon became the "Farmer's Bible." Up until then, farmers in the United States bought from village general stores where the selection was limited and prices high. Sears guaranteed the cheapest prices available anywhere, and orders poured in. Then the company moved to Chicago, the centre of mailing and rail shipping.

Sears Comes to Canada

Sears' ideas developed as he went along. There were no merchandising courses in those days. But he was a showman. He talked to farmers, the group that gave him the most business. He was said to be the world's largest retailer as sales were running into billions of dollars annually. Many disgruntled small-town merchants held bonfires where his catalogues were burned. Housewives who brought in their eggs and got twelve cents a dozen for them, providing they took it in merchandise, were often told by these store owners that they should try to sell their eggs to Richard Sears. But still Mr. Sears' business grew. He lived to be eighty-eight, and saw his company expand into Canada, where they now have seventy-five stores and eight hundred catalogue order offices from coast to coast. Annual sales in Canada topped four billion dollars in 1985.

The firm is still a Sears' operation. To think that the whole thing started because a jeweller decided he didn't want a dozen pocket watches because the shipment was late. It wasn't too late for Richard W. Sears!

5
It All Started in North Bay

It was back in 1932 and Roy K. Thomson was a wholesale radio salesman. He worked out of Ottawa and his salary was on commission, dependent upon the number of sets he sold. Hardware stores were the primary retailers of radio sets, and few people had them. The main reason was that most folks didn't have a hundred dollars to spare, which was the average price of a set.

One day Thomson took a train trip to North Bay, Ontario. He couldn't afford a car. He'd heard that most men up there were working in logging or mines and had money to spend. Moreover, there was probably a hardware store up north which would be interested in selling the excellent radio line he represented.

Thomson checked in at the hotel in North Bay, that charged three dollars a night for a room. Next day he visited the hardware dealer, who said that he'd be happy to handle the line, if he thought it would sell. Roy Thomson couldn't see any reason why sales shouldn't be good. People had plenty of free time in that cold winter area, and they were working and apparently had money — not like in Toronto and Montreal, where no one seemed to have any spare cash.

The dealer invited Thomson to spend a few days in town. Two of the sets were placed in the trunk of the dealer's car and they visited people who had called at the store and indicated interest in buying a set.

The sets were plugged in and turned on, but nothing much happened except a few buzzes, squawks, and whistles. They soon realized that this was because the nearest radio station was the CBC in Toronto, some two hundred and ten miles south.

Mr. Thomson agreed with the hardware man that they had a real problem. He knew now that the way to sell radios was to bring a station into North Bay. A great idea, thought Thomson, except that he had no money. He began checking around and asking questions, and soon heard that an electrical firm in Toronto had a low-power transmitter for sale for fifty dollars. He went off to Toronto and managed to buy it.

Back in North Bay he was able to get space over a local theatre. Apparently the theatre manager was given the opportunity to advertise his coming attractions, in exchange for a reduction in rent. There was also an engineer available to install the transmitter and other equipment. A few days before the station was opened, Thomson was out selling commercial time to local merchants for the opening day. He got a dollar or two a message, and even had the mayor make the introductory speech.

It was a great show and no doubt plenty of radios were sold. But now Thomson was more interested in this new business career he had unearthed. A career that developed because he had discovered a need and was now filling it.

In the following years he was to open more stations in the north country, as well as purchase newspapers across Canada, in the United States and overseas. He bought the prominent London *Times*, which was later sold. Roy Thomson was knighted. His family has since acquired the Toronto *Globe and Mail*, as well as various department stores such as Simpson's. But it was all started by a man who had little capital, but an idea he promoted.

6
It Started With Scones

The largest independent bakery in Canada, with more than one hundred trucks on the road, was started in Montreal by Dent Harrison in 1885.

Young Dent was eighteen and worked in a manufacturing plant as a labourer. There were a number of men in the plant who, like Dent, had recently come over from England, and were looking for an opportunity to make good. After all, the fare on a Canadian Pacific ship was only fifteen dollars. The line had recently been awarded a mail contract and so fares were cheap on the big ships that ploughed across the Atlantic in six days.

There was one thing that many of the workers missed, and that was the afternoon break they got back home, with tea and freshly-baked scones. While young Dent Harrison went about his duties he thought about the workers lament, "Why can't we have scones?"

He couldn't find anyone locally who baked them, but he knew someone back home who did! His grandmother in England would give him the recipe she was so proud of. He decided to pay her a visit; she was getting on in years. She didn't write many letters, and he wanted the recipe *immediately*. He was well aware that there's nothing hotter than an idea whose time has come!

So with less than fifty dollars he had saved, he took a boat back home. He was back in Canada within two weeks and promptly bought a three burner portable gas stove (in those days almost everyone cooked with gas). He set up the plate burner in his room and began experimenting with the baking of scones in his spare time. Since he had no training as a baker, he had to do his experimenting in the evenings because he was at work in the steel mill during the day.

When he thought his scones were equal to the kind his grandmother made, he bought a push cart and began calling on housewives in the area after work, and, of course, he took a supply to his co-workers. His scones were so good that there were never any left over. Nearby housewives began asking for this delicacy, and business was soon so brisk that Dent Harrison quit his job and bought a horse and wagon. He rented a small place to bake in, hired a helper, and soon added bread to his line.

By the year 1900, Harrison's yellow horse-drawn vehicles, bearing the name "Dent Harrison & Sons," could be seen all over the city of Montreal. In later years, three grandsons carried on the proud tradition grandfather had started now under the name of Harrison Brothers using the trade mark POM — Pride of Montreal. Another idea that grew!

7
Holiday Inn Empire Started with an Idea

In 1951 Kemmons Wilson and his family stayed at a Washington D.C. hotel. He was disgusted; the accommodation was cramped, and the rates were high for what he got. There was an extra room charge for the children, the meals were only fair, and they were expensive.

There was little for the family to do while he was busy with business calls.

He returned home and sat at his dining room table pondering what a hotel should offer the public to make it appealing and successful. Wilson believed that the world was ready to do a lot of travelling.

He considered large rooms to be an important feature — probably at least twenty-four feet long. He also wanted a hotel that didn't charge for children of twelve or under if they slept in the same room as their parents. Good meals available at reasonable prices were important, as well as a swimming pool where the family could lounge while the father made his business calls.

Although Wilson didn't have much money, he decided that it was a good idea that he should build such a hotel. Immediately, he called two or three friends and explained his idea to them. He said the hotel would be filling a need, "And if you fill a need with the right product or service you can't go wrong."

Wilson's enthusiasm was catching and his friends agreed to put some money into the idea. They decided that the location should not be right in town, but a little way out. This would mean lower land costs, easier parking, and other benefits.

Along with the available money, plus a good mortgage, Kemmons Wilson turned his idea into a reality; he became founder of the first Holiday Inn. It is said that the name came from the movie, which he had seen and liked.

The Holiday Inn prospered from the beginning, and soon people were clamoring for franchises. Before long, the name had spread world-wide and there were soon more than seventeen hundred inns bearing the name Holiday Inn. Today, there is hardly a city in Canada, the United States or other major countries around the world where you won't find a Holiday Inn. All because Kemmons Wilson was disgusted with a hotel in which he stayed.

8
It Pays to Be on Time

A salesman, holidaying in England, met a man who had a knitted sweater business. He had dozens of women working at home knitting sweaters which he sold to boutiques. It was a local cottage industry.

This sweater man, who was very proud of the work, asked the salesman to try to get business from retail shops in ski areas in Switzerland where the salesman operated. So the salesman took samples and made calls, and a few sales resulted. Then he heard of a new super-duper sportswear store that would be opening in two months. He got an order for five hundred heavy-duty sweaters that would sell well to skiers. The total value of the sale ran into thousands of dollars, and the salesman was very excited about the big commission cheque he would receive. "Don't forget," warned the customer, "we need them by the end of October at the latest."

"No problem," promised the salesman. He immediately phoned the order to the sweater man, who said he would have them by the required date.

The salesman became worried when six weeks had passed and the shipment hadn't arrived. He knew that the customer had already begun to advertise and had taken some advance orders for the sweaters. So he phoned England again and was assured that the cottage women were working overtime and the sweaters would arrive on time.

When the merchandise hadn't arrived three days before the store opening the salesman made another call.

"Got a surprise for you," said the sweater man. "I'm bringing the whole shipment over in my station wagon. It's jam-packed. The wife has never seen that part of the country so she'll enjoy it, and we may make a few side trips on the way."

The salesman implored the man to make his side trips on the return trip as there were barely three days left, and considerable distance was to be travelled. "Don't worry," said the man, "you'll have the goods on time."

The salesman was up at six the day the big store was to open. He watched and waited. The people poured into the place. He heard many of them ask to see the new line of sweaters. But the answer was always the same. "Sorry." At eight o'clock that night the weary salesman went to his hotel room and fell into bed. Next morning he didn't bother visiting the sportswear store.

It was four days later before the sweater-knitter stopped his dusty station wagon at the hotel and rang the salesman. "Come on down," he cried. "I've got a surprise for you. Got your entire order. Had a little car trouble, but better late than never! Where's the store." "*You'll* be surprised," said the salesman. " The store owner cancelled his order. Said he couldn't wait."

The moral is, when you promise a delivery date, be sure you keep it.

9
The Dog Food Man

A man had what he considered to be a brilliant idea. He would make up bags of good quality dog food and sell it through retail outlets in his town. He would do this work with the aid of one helper. He had a dog, often bought food, and read the ads in magazines and newspapers for dog food, so figured he was an expert.

He mixed a considerable batch of his food in dried form, buying the ingredients from a firm who produced these as a by-product.

He then loaded his station wagon with his product and called on local stores. He made out very well with independents, but found he had to approach the head offices of the two chain prospects in town. He figured that he could control about half the dog food sales in town with the representation he had. Of course the stores would only take his line on a consignment basis. They'd pay when the product sold. This was the man's first venture into business and he was learning the rules *after* starting instead of before.

The Big Blitz

He planned to run a half page ad in each of the two local papers, offering his product at a low price as an introductory deal. He got advance proofs of the ads and sent them off to the head offices of the chains, and used the same ad copies to crack a couple of the local stores which hadn't purchased his product.

He figured he'd move to other towns as business grew. He had started with three thousand dollars, and had so far spent twenty-five hundred of this on printed bags, ingredients, stationery, and his forthcoming ads.

Then the day dawned on which the big sale was to start. The ads appeared in the papers. Even the radio ran a blurb. It was with great glee that he bought the papers and went through them expectantly. But his excitement turned to amazement when he discovered that he wasn't the only dog food advertiser offering a special price!

Two of his big, national competitors had apparently heard of his invasion into their territory and had countered with ads twice the size of his and a week-long special price at a third of his!

It had been a simple job for the competitors. They had been advised by their sales people in the area of an intrusion by a new competitor. So all they did was to take an old ad and reduce the price! The new dog food man realized that his competition had discovered his entry into the marketplace, and that this information might have come from one of the local papers or from a dealer stocking his line.

The well-known brands sold wildly, while the new man's product sales languished. His entry into business was a dismal failure. The national companies had spent a lot of money introducing their lines into the area and they weren't going to take any chance of a new competitor reducing their sales.

If the new dog food man had learned something about his competition, he probably would not have chosen such a highly competitive business.

This is an extreme example, but it does show the value of good market surveys.

Research and Marketing

To be successful in business, you need a good idea, and then you set to work to carry it out. Once you have what you believe is something the public will be interested in, it is best to do some research and marketing work. As a small beginner it is wise to do this work yourself, otherwise you'll receive a great stack of reports from research people who make their living conducting surveys. You will no doubt have to provide the questions the pollsters will ask. But you can always change the questions to suit the area and the occasion if you do the work yourself, and of course, it's much cheaper and more reliable.

We'll assume you have decided on the type of business you will conduct. Will you offer a product or a service? A service business, such as a janitorial operation, doesn't require an investment in products for resale, although you do have to buy working equipment.

The Right Questions

You will have to look at your competition. Do they operate from a store or office, or is it a one-person spare-time home operation? Is there any special service, such as delivery? Do they advertise and what are their prices? Do they project a good image? All this should give you some indication of what's happening in the marketplace.

Can you offer better prices, a better product, or service? Will you have to advertise or use publicity to attract business? Is location important and, if so, how will the location you have, or hope to have, compare with your competition?

The Local Survey

Before starting even the smallest business it is wise to conduct a survey. It is not wise to send out letters and sit back waiting for answers. Most people just couldn't be bothered. It is better to make a few phone calls, or even call on people in your area. You may not be guided by what they say, but you could pick up some valuable information.

One woman was going to open a small "home-made" bakery. There had already been a bakery in the spot where she intended to open. The previous owner had done well for the first three months and then had gone under. The new baker discovered that the previous owner had gone under for two reasons. The first was that he let his quality deteriorate after he figured he had a steady flow of customers. He was all excited about his big profits. Secondly, there was a little extra space in the store and some people had suggested that he handle some convenience store items, such as soft drinks, candies, cigarettes, and newspapers. Soon there was a gang hanging around the place and the bakery business was finished. At last he stopped baking, and he put in a complete line of convenience store products. This didn't work and the store soon closed.

This was interesting news to the new baker, some of whose potential customers also suggested that a little sideline, such as hot coffee, sandwiches and cakes, would be a welcome and needed service.

In a week the survey was completed and the store was eventually opened according to the suggestions. Now, after two years, the business is doing very well.

Money Making Suggestions

Sound, practical ideas are important if you want to cash in on them. You will note in the preceding case histories that each business person had a good idea to start with. It's also much easier to raise money, if you have to, when you have a workable idea.

What is a Good Idea?

In business, a good idea is generally a product or service that is either needed or created when people start using the product or service. As you no doubt noted in the previous pages, simple ideas are often the ones that result in the most success.

Professor Hires was a chemist and one day he gathered two or three natural roots and developed his well known drink. Obviously it was a difficult thing to promote. What could you call it? A friend suggested that a lot of people like beer. How about a name like Hires Root Beer? And the name was born.

Of course it also happens that some people have ideas that for some reason aren't successful.

Years ago Ford Motors introduced their Edsel automobile. It was said to be very advanced, and was named after a grandson of Henry Ford, who invented the automobile. Research programs had been carried out, people were interviewed, and there was great enthusiasm. A fortune was spent advertising the new car, but the Edsel didn't catch on. In a couple of years, the car was off the market, and today the few you'll find are collectors' treasures.

What follows are a series of money-making ideas for the ambitious person. Many can be done in spare time, and most require only very little capital to start. You might find just the plan you've been looking for or an idea that might lead to something else.

What you choose could be the beginning of something worthwhile. Who knows? Maybe you'll be laying the groundwork for a worldwide empire.

1
Prints from Europe

Prints from overseas are worth considering as a part-time business. One of the better purchase areas is France, where very colourful prints can be had for around five dollars each, wholesale. Prints of scenes in Paris and Cannes are extremely popular. With an inexpensive glass frame you can get twenty to twenty-five dollars each at retail. Prints of many European cities are available, and mailing costs are low because a one-pound package can contain many prints. There is usually a small duty on these imports.

Hotels and offices are good markets for prints of this type. In addition to local sales you could consider mail-order, though I would suggest you try the home market — maybe two or three cities — first. Hiring salespeople to handle your line could be profitable. Boutiques are worth considering. When working out a selling price charge four times your cost price. In your costs, include print, frame, shipping, and duty. So, if seven dollars is your cost, your retail price should be twenty-five to twenty-eight dollars. Large prints for office buildings could retail at up to fifty dollars.

You should try various countries for information regarding prints. You could contact the Chamber of Commerce in major cities of the countries you are interested in. They should be able to provide you with a list of wholesale sources. Or you can write or phone their Consulates in Ottawa or in Washington, D.C. They might have the names of suppliers.

2
Church Histories Work Out Well

Almost all churches have a history worth preserving, and publishing them can be an excellent part-time occupation providing the church approves the idea.

Some large United States consultancy firms are turning out very elaborate books of this type. They contain a history of the church from the time it was founded, photos of the building and often of many of the dignitaries who have been associated with the church and its work over the years. These books usually have hard covers and are printed on excellent paper. The retail cost per book runs up to twenty dollars a copy.

Usually the church can supply a knowledgable person to gather photos and information for the book. The writing, arrangement of photos and layout of the book can either be done by you or by an outside professional.

Quantity and Pricing

The quantity printed will depend on the size of the church's congregation. If it is five hundred, then seven hundred and fifty copies should be printed to make up for unexpected orders, church reserves, and so on. So, if your print costs run around two thousand dollars or more, you should arrange to get a sizable advance as the printer will expect immediate payment. You would need to check with different printers for prices, and get written quotations for the job before the work starts. This will prevent any unexpected charges later on.

Your primary source of income will probably be the congregation, but you can't always predict the number of people who will buy. To estimate your retail price, you should double or triple the price of your print cost per book. So, if your price is five dollars, then your selling price would be ten to fifteen dollars a copy. The total cost could be substantial, so you might ask the church leaders to help you find sponsorship. You ask the church to buy a substantial number of copies in addition to sales to parishioners. Sometimes church people will give a substantial donation in exchange for having their name published in the book as a donor, or in memory of a loved one.

A worthwhile, attractive book can be very profitable if the advance work is done properly and the church agrees on an up-front payment to at least cover the out-of-pocket costs.

3
Food Specialists

An interesting line of products that can be handled in spare hours, both locally and/or by mail, is specialty foods. You can choose from candies, cakes, hams, local maple syrup, jams, jellies, nuts, fruit, or other delicacies. When you prepare an order, include a list, possibly with enticing photos, of other products you may offer.

Some spare-time operators have graduated to full-time and have become very big in this business. Your best source of suppliers are firms experienced in producing and packing the kind of food you are interested in. There are such things as correct packing and shipping, so that your product won't spoil or be damaged when shipped. There are also certain regulations regarding the preparation of foods, which should be left to people experienced in this work.

You may want your own label on foods, but area regulations could demand that the city where the food has been prepared and packed must appear on the label. This might read: John Doe, Packer, XYZ CITY, etc., for your name, purveyors of Specialty Foods, address. It might be necessary to list the manufacturer's name and address, but checking will provide you with these details.

4
Is the Mail-Order Business For You?

Selling by mail is a wonderful idea. You just sit at your desk or kitchen table, open the batch of envelopes the post office just delivered, and remove the cheques, money orders, and cash. Yes, mail order is a wonderful idea. But it doesn't always pay off, as many people who have tried have learned.

There are many problems in this business that pertain to no other operation. On the other hand, mail-order can be fascinating and profitable. There are many stories about those who made it big as well as those who went under. Much of the time the operator can't really tell which way the wind will blow. Let's take a look at a successful mail-order story.

Hamburger Pays Off

There is the story of one man who heard his wife remark, when things weren't going very well, "The family must be tired of plain hamburger — bet I know fifty ways of cooking it!"

Her statement gave her husband an idea: Why not prepare a booklet containing all the ways of preparing hamburger, and advertise it at three dollars a copy?

According to the story, this entrepreneur placed small classified ads in three United States magazines with big circulations. Apparently readers were very interested in how they could cook tasty hamburger in fifty different ways, because those three dollar cheques just rolled in. He first printed five hundred copies of his twelve page booklet, but soon went back to press.

Basic Mail-Order Steps

This man had learned some important things about mail-order. He had learned that you have to fill a need, and that you can't sell something by mail that every corner store has. It should be a product that doesn't get damaged in shipping, is light in weight to keep postage low, and, gets results from classified ads. Also, a low purchase price is essential. People don't know you, so may not trust you, but they'll gamble for a couple of dollars. Another important thing is that classified ads cost money. Many of the larger magazines charge five to twenty-five dollars a word, with a minimum of ten words. This includes your address, as well as your name, so it is wise to use as few words as possible.

Another important thing is to have a second circular you can include with every order shipped. Now your customer has bought from you, he can trust you and you can expect a larger order on your next offer.

In mail-order it is best if you actually produce your own product. This way you have control of costs and date of delivery.

Printed Material Sells Better

Mail-order people feel that the cost of their product should be at least one in six. By that I mean that if a booklet is thirty-two pages long, and costs you fifty cents to print, a fair retail price would be between three and four dollars. This is necessary because of advertising, postage, addressing, and wrapping costs.

Mail-Order Meetings

People in the business have associations that meet regularly, where they tell stories about their latest business adventures. Even people in the business for a half century are often surprised by the results — or lack of them.

A Montreal man, long experienced in mail-order while living in the United States, was approached by a manufacturer and publicity person to discuss a new product that they thought was certain to be a great seller.

The climate in their area was extremely warm and the product was a unit that kept the bed cool. It sold for around fifty dollars. The mail-order man was excited when he discovered that it worked as reported. He took full page ads in a number of local daily newspapers to advertise the item during one of the hottest summers for years. The advertiser had dozens of units packaged, ready to have an address label put on as soon as the orders came in. Did they come in? After one week the total was three; just over one hundred and fifty dollars worth. The cost of the ads was over ten thousand dollars!

Later the inventor placed the item in department stores and it sold well. Why? First, the customers could examine the product;

secondly, they could buy it on the store's charge system if they wished; and thirdly, they could return it easily if they didn't want it.

Then of course there are stories of great successes.

How Major Mail-Order Advertisers Work

There are a number of ways large mail-order advertisers go after business. They buy lists of names and addresses, paying up to fifty dollars per thousand labels, and sometimes even more. Your name is valuable. If you buy from some companies, a list broker will probably buy your name and then re-sell it with thousands of other names. Classified and larger space advertisers often sell fresh or new names to brokers who in turn sell to other advertisers.

Many magazines and/or publishers rent their list of subscribers rather than sell them. In this process the advertiser may send their offer-filled envelopes to the publisher who will postage-meter the mail and address it. But at no time does the advertiser see copies of the list, because the publisher doesn't want competitors to get their hands on it. As the publisher or magazine decides who will be allowed to rent the list, they will require prior approval of your mailing offer before agreeing to a deal. Thus, they are assured that they are not dealing with a competitor.

Big firms in the business of selling by mail often publish catalogues, and sometimes have catalogue order stores in many communities.

The Importance of Keying

When you place an ad, it is wise to "key it." This means you put an identifying word or letter in your return address in a specific classified ad or display, so you will know where your orders or inquiries are coming from.

If you are a big advertiser you might use such terms as "Desk 16," the number identifying the magazine in which your ad was placed and the business that results. But the small classified advertiser, if his address number is 100 might use 100A. This letter would cost nothing extra. The letter A might stand for *Avalanche* if there was such a magazine and you were using it. Or you might key it as "100-1," the figure *1* being your code for a publication. Make sure there is no 1001 on your street, and if there is no South, West, East or North, 100-S is good. Many magazine readers are well aware of this little keying trick and may leave off your code number, but no one leaves off S or N as it could be a part of your address. You could also use 100-AJ. The J standing for the month your ad appears, if you are running more than one ad. It shouldn't affect postal services.

Writing Short Ads

There are individuals who specialize in writing classified ads. If you run an ad you will receive letters of all kinds, and some, no doubt, will be from people who will tell you how they would improve your ad for a fee. They might, too!

Many Amateurs Overwrite

In classifieds, many new advertisers use words that aren't necessary. If you're paying seven dollars a word, three or four extra words can cost you money, especially if you are running the ad more than once.

You can often tell the work of an amateur. They may use words such as *please*, or *postage paid* instead of *postpaid*. Or they may add, *for free information write* . . . Obviously people are not actually going to show up personally for free information, so the single word *Details*, or *Information* followed by the address will do, and will save you three precious words.

A while back, I had some booklets on mail-order that I wanted to sell at five dollars each. I knew that an offer advertising the booklet outright by classified ad wouldn't pull very much business. So I prepared this little classified: "Get mail-order cheques daily! Details!" — plus the address.

The ad copy came to five words, yet told everything. It was also placed under one of the free headings most magazines offer. I chose "Mail-Order Opportunities." Many magazines offer a choice of dozens of headings. Total wordage, including the address, was ten. The ad ran twice at a total cost of about seventy-five dollars. The total number of inquiries was a hundred and ten. This was around sixty-five cents an inquiry. This ad appeared in *Popular Mechanics*.

Some advertisers say they have paid as little as a quarter per inquiry. But I doubt that this happens very often with specific-type ads. Specific ads ask for inquiries from the kind of reader likely to be interested in your offer — for instance " Old Books Available." A general ad could be "Make big profits! Free Information!" This type of ad pulls heavily, but sales results could still be low. *Popular Mechanics* has a paid circulation of about one million, eight hundred thousand, and reports four readers per issue for a total readership of almost eight million per month. When I talked to them on the phone, they said they figured my returns were good.

Paid for Ad

From the hundred and ten inquiries that came in from all over the world, I was able to receive enough orders to pay for the ad. I enclosed an additional circular with every order I fulfilled — definitely a cheaper way to advertise and who knows, a few people might reorder. This is what is called "piggyback" in the trade.

You have to experiment with mail-order, and if it works you can assume that you are on the right track.

5
Getting Into Broadcasting

In the past, a good voice was the main requirement. It's still important for men to have a deep voice — known as a golden voice — and for women, a clear, strong, "musical" voice. But now, radio and television are looking for experienced people who know what they are doing. Experience gained from a junior college program with courses in broadcasting and journalism, or a school that specializes in it, is very helpful.

Knowledge of business, economics, history, sociology, politics and geography are important, especially the way talk shows are developing. A lot of DJ's find their work a twenty-four-hour-a-day job. They listen to other stations to hear what's happening elsewhere. They are voracious readers so they can keep up with things in general, as well as to get new ideas.

Some stations use part-time help to handle interview shows in off-times, such as mid-afternoon. Sometimes college teachers and sports celebrities can get on the air at regular hours.

Major Markets

Experienced people come into a major market and do a good, clean show without making mistakes.

Many hopefuls send in demo tapes to radio stations, and this can be helpful. Probably a demo won't get you an immediate job offer, but it could result in an interview. Busy Program Directors don't appreciate it when someone walks through the front door demanding a job. Radio stations are busy places. It's easier to mail your demo tape and let executives listen at their leisure. Make a short tape, stating your name, phone number, address, and experience at the beginning of the tape and repeat your name, address and phone number at the end. Do a couple of commercials and some news items.

There are about six hundred radio stations in Canada and eight thousand in the United States. Almost all libraries have directories of the names and addresses of these stations. Small towns offer the best opportunities because they are not considered a major market, thus not attractive to a lot of broadcasting professionals.

Getting on TV

Many TV announcers and show hosts come from radio, and radio people are often newspaper columnists holding down two jobs. This is often the case with writers of specialty columns reporting on sports, lifestyles, children, cars, and business, as well as other topics.

Because getting on radio usually takes time, other "in between" jobs are advisable while you wait for the big break.

Want to Buy a Station?

Many ambitious people think owning a radio station costs a fortune. This is not necessarily so. A small station (AM) can run on just one to two thousand watt power and could broadcast a strong signal for an area of about twenty-five to thirty miles.

Small stations don't usually make big money. Big stations are often part of a chain, or network.

Small stations have few employees, generally because the boss — usually the owner — can only afford to hire three or four people. Among other jobs the staff may be required to do announcing, sell advertising, collect bills, clean up, interview people and cover special events.

Small stations do come up for sale from time to time. The big stations are not usually interested because the smaller stations are not big money-makers. Sometimes a small station owner wants to retire. There is often no real estate involved. Stations of all sizes frequently rent their quarters.

If you're hard-working and reliable, you might be able to buy a station with a very small down payment and a monthly payment. People have purchased small stations for as little as two to five thousand dollars down, and monthly payments of five hundred dollars or less. The seller is getting what he considers to be the best deal possible and so he won't squeeze the buyer. It's much better to get an assured small down payment and regular monthly fee (often a percentage of income) than to force a buyer to make payments which aren't in line with the station's income.

It's similar to my experience in the magazine business. Over the years I have bought at least six magazines for a couple of hundred dollars or less. In each case the previous owner wasn't making big money. Sometimes they grossed thirty thousand dollars a year, with expenses of twenty-five thousand dollars. There might be obligations, such as contracts, etc., which the seller wants the new owner to continue. In my cases, I was able to build up some of these magazines and sell them for fifty thousand dollars or more.

The same principle applies to radio. Read the trade journals, such as *Broadcaster* in Canada, at 7 Labatt Street, Toronto, Ontario, M5A 3P2, and *U.S. Broadcasting*, at 1735 DeSales Street, N.W., Washington, D.C. 20036. These publications will not only keep you abreast of opportunities, but will also initiate you into the business.

6
Want to Import Merchandise?

At some point you've probably looked at exotic products from such places as Taiwan, and other overseas countries. Maybe you could sell such items to your friends, or by mail. You've checked mail-order ads seeking sales people for these items; their ads inform you of the fortune that Suzie Clutz made last year. Maybe you can make even more money by being your own importer.

If you are really interested, the easiest way to get information is by contacting the consulate of that country in Ottawa if you live in Canada, and in Washington, D.C., if you reside in the United States. If, for example, you wanted to inquire about Italian leather goods, you would ask directory information for the number of the Italian Consulate in Ottawa. The consulates and embassies of most countries maintain trade offices around the world and they will be happy to help you. Should the consulate not have the data you require, they will put you in touch with the department that *does* have such information, and these people will help you out with names, addresses, types of goods, etc.

What you must remember is that most countries spend a lot of money to promote their merchandise abroad. Just as Canada and the United States maintain trade offices in most countries, a foreign office may spend twenty-five dollars or more just to obtain, and pass on to you, catalogues and other information about their country's specialities.

Importing: it's interesting, exciting, and could be profitable. You decide.

Exchange, Shipping, and Delivery

If you do decide to buy from another country, check their exchange regulations. Many firms demand payment in U.S. funds, or its equivalent. Thus a very low-priced product can become high-priced. Also you may have to buy in very large quantities to get a good deal. Almost every out-of-the-country company wants cash up front. Then of course there's the cost of transportation, which would be by sea or by land, not air. Also, make sure you get a sample of the product you are interested in.

Next, you'll have to get a broker to look after your interests. You will have to pay him, and there could also be tax or other charges imposed by your own government. There is also a possibility of damage and late delivery.

I once bought a large quantity of good quality hunting knives from a Montreal importer, who had followed every rule and regulation practiced by the experienced importer. The goods were supposed to arrive in Montreal by May at the latest for distribution to stores in time for the coming hunting season — starting in some areas in September. The importer figured he had plenty of time.

The shipment came from the Far East via London — all very proper. It had to be re-shipped, often standard. But suddenly there was a dock strike in Britain. This importer finally got his merchandise in October! The knives were supposed to sell at six dollars each, and would wholesale at about half this. The importer was stuck with thousands of hunting knives, which he'd paid for in advance.

I contacted him and he offered me all I wanted at a dollar each for cash. I bought about three hundred and took them to the *Toronto Sportsmen's Show* which ran in March. I offered them, as a pitchman, at five dollars each, explaining exactly what had happened. People lined up at my booth, and I was able to sell out. Everyone won except the importer.

Still Want to Handle Imports?

The easiest way is to go to a local importer already importing the merchandise you wish to sell. In this manner, you become a wholesaler. You'll probably have to go to a large city to find one. Look in the phone book (yellow pages) under "Importers." Different importers usually handle different products, which they sell to retailers. They buy and stock huge quantities. Many have display rooms, where you can walk around and examine and price merchandise. You won't have to worry about money exchange, late deliveries, wrong merchandise, damage, etc. For all of this you might pay a few pennies more. These people buy in quantity and will sell to you in small lots, if that's the way you want it. You could do all right this way, even when selling at less than the suggested retail price to schools, churches and other groups. These groups, in turn, can resell them to raise money for their activities.

7
The Real Estate Boom

Across the land in towns and cities there are evening talks taking place that tell you how to make a fortune in real estate, usually with no money down. These super-slick lecturers come into a city, rent a hotel lecture hall — the cost of which averages forty dollars for one hundred chairs, and includes either a lectern or table — and probably a microphone.

These operators like to choose a Monday or Thursday night, because they seem to be more productive in terms of the number of people who show up and the number of books or courses sold. The price of these courses may run up to three hundred dollars. The person sponsoring the event (usually the speaker), often reports a nightly profit of five thousand dollars or more.

These people are almost always men, and they are spellbinders. They are positive, dynamic, forceful, and know all about making money in real estate with no money down. However, it has been said that they make the most money from telling their paying guests how to do it.

Getting the Crowds

So, the Hoopla boys now have a hall, and all they need are the crowds. This is easily arranged. A half-dozen radio commercials and an ad or two in the local paper will do the trick. The operator will also hire an attractive woman or two (or they may be part of the troupe) to hand out folders at the entrance to the hall. Their talks are usually well-attended. Everyone wants to know how it's done, and excited guests anxiously wait for the night of the big event.

These operators must be related to the fellows who conducted "get rich quick" schemes on the river boats a hundred or more years ago.

The Sales Pitch

The slick salesman may start off with a sly, humourous remark such as, "Those who are not interested in making big money fast may leave now if they wish to avoid being bored." This is designed to relax the audience.

Next the operator will tell you how he has made two or three quick fortunes in the business, implying that he is just giving these talks to pass the time.

The speaker will then explain how his course can help you do the same thing. Those genuinely in the real estate business say that all of this is perfectly legitimate, but only few people are able to take advantage of today's billowing real estate market, which is often paralleled to the old "gold rush" days.

The Changing World of Real Estate

During the past few years everyone has heard tales of houses that have sold for as much as a half-dozen times what they cost when built. Houses that cost twenty thousand dollars fifteen or twenty years ago seem to bring all kinds of high prices today. Of course there are some "soft spots" around the country, and this is where money can be made — in speculation. (A "soft spot" occurs when real estate prices fall and investors can buy property and resell later, when prices have risen.) The trouble with real estate speculation is that one never knows if a "soft spot" will get softer, tying up your hard-earned capital in a fixed asset that you cannot quickly sell.

In today's market, it's a fact that whenever interest rates on mortgages go down, house sales show an increase. Other prime factors in the rise of house prices are ever-increasing rents for tenants, less available land near cities, and increasing labour and construction material costs.

The Handyman's Special

An older house, even if it's run-down, can often be a good buy, especially for someone handy with tools. I know a railway man whose hobby is buying old houses, repairing and selling them. He makes more money at this than he does at his job.

You rarely find old, run-down houses in relatively new neighbourhoods, but there are two kinds of "new" neighbourhoods. One is a completely new housing development where a developer has taken over a large piece of land such as a golf-course, an offshore island or something of that nature. Real estate prices can be high here, and so can taxes, as all services are new. As initial purchase prices are likely to be high in these areas any investment here could take some time before it paid off.

The second kind of new neighbourhood is the expansion of older areas. These areas are becoming popular again for many reasons; suburban areas because of improved highways or other forms of transportation, lower taxes, community feeling, etc. In these areas, vacant lots are quickly built on, and older houses are bought, demolished and new structures built to replace them, or quickly renovated and resold.

Contact Real Estate People

Advise real estate agents that you are interested in purchasing older properties; it may put you first in line for bargains. Also, keep a close watch on the area yourself. It sometimes happens that residents, after many years in a home, want to sell out and move to a condominium or apartment. Very often a place like this can be bought with little up-front money.

Checking House Repairs

The life of a furnace is twenty years maximum. A roof is about the same. Unless plumbing pipes are copper there could be a five to ten thousand dollar repair bill. Then there could be expensive exterior repairs such as crumbling brickwork or wood deterioration, among other things. If the oil tank is the same age as the furnace it could be leaking. Was it installed before all basement walls were completed? It could be costly to have to remove a section of wall to install your new two hundred gallon fuel tank.

However, a piece of property that you own and live in is almost always a great investment. You are not at a landlord's beck and call every time there is a tax increase, nor are you subject to other problems, such as increasing rents, which are so prevalent when you are leasing. And there are always bargains in real estate if you can keep a weather-eye open.

8
The Kitchen-Table Publisher

Writers, poets, artists, and other ambitious people who write booklets that they find difficult to get published might consider what is called kitchen-table publishing. This can be a small, inexpensive operation, but it can be very profitable. This is true of poetry, short stories, biographies, self-help, and many other types of booklets. Self-publishing is a business that has become very popular because of today's fast-changing publishing and distribution set-up.

Some people in the above categories are publishing their own work, and selling it successfully. One woman published five hundred copies of a poetry booklet and sold four hundred copies to friends, poetry club members, and other groups. These sales more than paid the cost of printing the booklet.

The Way to Start

Let's assume you have written something you want to publish. Your first step is to set it in type. This should be a home operation, otherwise the cost of outside typesetting could be a big expense.

To set type you need a typewriter. But no ordinary typewriter will do. Even if you have what appears to be a fair machine, it probably won't give the professional look you want. You need a machine that will type really black characters in a business-like "face." Your best bet is to rent a typewriter that uses a black carbon ribbon. Choose a machine that has a typeface that resembles what you might find in a magazine or book. If you can't locate a machine that uses a carbon ribbon, then at least choose a typewriter that has a face you'll be happy with when the job is done.

If you'd prefer to use a computer, you will probably have to experiment. What you don't want is a machine that gives you grey type with parts of letters missing. On the other hand, if you have your copy done by a professional typesetting shop, it could cost you twenty dollars a page or more, so it pays to do the job yourself. If you are not a professional typist, then hire a spare-time typist to do the work for you.

Getting Ready for the Copy Centre

Your next step is to choose a printer. I am referring to what is known as a copy centre. These can be found in all cities and many towns. They are inexpensive and fast. On a small run — say five hundred copies of a thirty-two page booklet — they could have your work ready in a couple of days.

They will print from paper (oxidized) plates made from your originals. They will print on standard white paper stock, usually known as forty pound 8½" x 11". They will not do typesetting unless you pay extra. Copy centres are primarily fast printers, often called photocopiers. These people are not to be confused with regular printers who charge more and turn out a high-quality product. Your work should be easy to read, and sharp. Even if you used whiteout or Scotch-taped certain paragraphs over the original work, it shouldn't show on the printing.

The printer will also print a cover for you. This should be on heavier paper stock than the interior. A white cover is fine. Cover stock is a little more expensive than the regular white pages you are using.

Almost all copy centres will give you a sheet showing their printing prices. This is for straight printing. You are supplying ready-to-print material, so should know your costs in advance.

You probably won't get as professional-looking a job as you might from a standard printer. However, you will be paying about one-third less.

What Will It Cost?

Remember that your copy centre won't give you any sharper work than your original copy, so don't expect miracles, and be sure to make any corrections before going to press.

I checked with three copy centres while writing this book, and found that they all charged about twenty-five dollars a page for printing five hundred two sided copies of an 8½" x 11" sheet.

For a booklet, you are better to go to "digest" size. This means you type a page (8½" x 11") sideways so you have two 8½" x 5½" pages per sheet. So for the twenty-five dollars mentioned, you will get four digest size pages. This works out at six dollars and twenty-five cents a digest page, plus folding, as it will be necessary for your printer to fold these pages on a special folding machine. You will type your work on just one side of the paper and you can clip two pages together on a plain sheet (not stapled) so he will know which backs up onto what. A little practice will set you right on this process. It is a good idea to make contact with a copy centre ahead of time to tell them what you intend to do. They may suggest some worthwhile tips about how they would like the work, how long they will take to print, and they may give you copies of booklets to show what a finished job will look like and how page numbering is done.

Art Ability Handy

You also need to paste up your front cover, and for this it would be best if you were an artist or had a friend who was. Don't give the printer a hodge-podge of artwork of different sizes. Using rubber cement, paste any artwork exactly the way you wish it to appear in the finished job. If your cover layout is larger (or smaller) than it should be on the finished cover, then your printer will charge you for reducing or enlarging it.

For your booklet title and any larger headings inside, you can always get paste-up letters from a stationery or art store. You can get a package of letters in different faces and sizes for around ten dollars.

You are better to publish in booklet (digest) size as you will have a unit easier to work with and mail. Libraries usually regard a publication of up to fifty or sixty pages as a booklet, and over that as a book.

Collating Your Work

So your copy shop has printed your work and put it in two or three cartons. Usually these people don't deliver so you must get it home yourself. You will check that the 8½" x 11" sheets are all folded.

Now begins your big job. You must spread the sheets out on a fair-size table or large desk. The sections should run 1-3-5-7-9-11-13-15. This will give you a total of thirty-two pages, including the cover, this being the total number of pages you decided on.

So you make up the booklet. Now you have to centre-staple it — usually with two staples. For this you will need the type of stapler that allows you to staple in the centre of the booklet. A standard stapler won't do.

Here you have choices. You can use a V-shaped stapler, a long-arm stapler, or even a foot operated or electrical stapler. I mention these choices because these are what you will likely be shown if you visit a firm which specializes in stapling equipment. Some stationery suppliers also have a good choice of machines.

The V-shaped unit is the lowest priced, also the easiest to use. It may run up to seventy-five dollars depending on the brand. This type usually uses special staples. The V-type is effective on a booklet of up to about sixty pages. The long-arm unit may run to just over a hundred dollars, but is heavy-duty and is less likely to break down when subject to consistent use.

Maybe it would be best to borrow or rent a machine for your first job. You could collate all your booklets and take them back to your printer for stapling, but this can be expensive, time-consuming, and fraught with problems in a busy shop. Also, when you've stapled your own booklet, you'll be able to look at it and say, "I did that!"

So let's say you have produced a thirty-two page booklet, and the total price for five hundred copies is two hundred and fifty dollars for printing, cover stock, and folding (this does not include your typesetting cost or any special letters you bought from the art shop or stationery store). The cost for printing would be around fifty cents a copy. On the basis of selling it at two and a half to three dollars a copy, your five hundred copies would bring you a thousand dollars, or more. This is assuming that all booklets are sold at the retail price, and that all are sold.

If you wish to reprint, your production costs won't change much. Copy centres offer very small reductions on larger runs. However, you can use your original copy, after making any necessary changes. Self-publishing can be a very interesting spare-time business.

9
You Can Become A Booklet Publisher

Small publishers, who have studied this business, frequently do well putting out booklets in their spare hours.

Among the type of booklets you might consider publishing are informational "How To's," for which there are hundreds of subjects. Some of the more popular are gardening, lawn-care, swimming, child-care, housekeeping, cooking, business, buying or selling a house, various phases of writing, car care, photography, games, stamps, coins, travel, history, boating, fishing, hunting, camping, carpentry, clothing, art, and house repairs.

Demand for Booklets

There is a definite need for booklets. A survey conducted by a New York publisher showed that only about four percent of the population ever visits bookstores. In order to deal with this problem, some paperback publishers have invaded the supermarkets, but they seldom offer "How-To" booklets.

However, since large firms — oil, automotive, and construction business — have taken over publishing houses, the whole aura of publishing has changed. These people are big business. Many a writer is rejected, not because the book won't sell in the home market, but because sales people have determined that it won't get an international sale.

It is also becoming more difficult for small publishers to get their product into chain book stores, or get adequate length of sales time for it. For publishers there is also the problem of book returns.

Book Publishing Problems

In Canada and the United States, stores can return unsold books for a full credit. This is generally not so in England, where stores buy only the number of titles they feel they can sell. In England, libraries are the big buyers of books. If a publisher gets a good library sale for a book, this title could be a bestseller. Store sales are secondary.

A friend of mine in Canada got his book distributed in England, and he arranged to lecture in a number of cities. After one such talk, he visited local book stores to see how his book was going. Almost invariably he got the same answer, "Oh, we had two copies. We sold them a month ago but didn't bother to re-order."

Canadian and American bookstores often load up their shelves with titles they feel will move, and with rising costs, publishers are not prone to gamble on books they feel may not do well. Booklets are often lost in the scramble.

The Small Publisher Arises

There are now dozens of small publishers who write, and publish their own fact booklets. However, a publisher doesn't have to be a writer to produce a book. He or she could contact a writing group, suggest a topic, and one of the group would take it from there. Payment is usually on a ten percent of sales basis, with a small advance.

There are stories of self-publishers who own a half-dozen cars and have houses in different parts of the country. You can see their full page ads in newspapers and magazines. A whole new world of classified ad pages has arisen as a result of this new breed of publisher. All this proves that there is a tremendous demand for informative booklets. Most of these booklets have been made possible by the small instant photocopying service, which has emerged as a result of new inventions in simple, inexpensive plate making. This is primarily a shift from older methods where a one-page aluminum plate (which cost about four dollars and took time to make) was superseded by an oxide-coated paper plate good for a run up to three thousand copies. These can be made instantly, and cost less than a dollar.

A popular size for a booklet is about forty to sixty pages. The overall cost to the publisher of a booklet should be about seventy-five cents to a dollar, with the sales price at four to six dollars. Five dollars is a good price because buyers will often slip a five dollar bill into an envelope, rather than bother writing a cheque. It is wise to send out a circular, advertising your other available booklets. "You give readers a choice," says one successful booklet publisher, "and they'll buy something."

Readers of "How-To" booklets are loyal buyers if you have enough topics to interest them. However, if you hit a slow-mover, and this happens to every publisher, there are certain steps you can take.

One publisher of booklets never prints a title until the orders start to flow in. If he does an initial ad program, a few inquiry-type classified ads, and there seems to be little interest, he may offer the inquiries and type-set pages at low cost to a fellow publisher. Alternatively, he could just send out another circular listing the selection of booklets he has. If he receives money, he could make photocopies of the set pages and send these instead.

Turning a Booklet into a Course

There is a story about one person who had two or three booklets on piano tuning. Anyone who has tried to have a piano tuned knows it can be difficult to find someone to do the job.

The small publisher discovered that not only were his booklets going well, but that people wanted further information. So he produced a course with a number of instruction booklets. He increased his price to three hundred dollars, payable in cash, or at thirty dollars per month for ten months, with a fifty dollar down payment. Last time I heard, his business was going well.

The main thing in a successful booklet or continuing course is to establish that there is a need for what you're offering. Getting an enthusiastic response to free information circulars is one way of doing this. Another is to give talks at clubs and association meetings. It is better to become part of the parade than to sit on the sidelines.

Publishing is growing all the time, and, if you really like the idea, it is well worth considering as a means of making a part-time or full-time income.

If you do produce a booklet, you might send a copy to The H.W. Wilson Company, 950 University Avenue, Bronx, New York 10452. They send out a monthly magazine to almost all libraries in the United States and Canada and give listings with the prices and titles published in what is called the Vertical File Index. There is no charge for this service, and you might get orders from libraries in both countries.

10
The Franchise Business

The franchise business, as we know it, was said to have been started in Canada and the United States by the Singer Sewing Machine Company in about 1860. A dealer was appointed in a city or town to open a store which sold and serviced Singer sewing machines exclusively. The franchisee operated his own store, paid any staff, and bought sewing machines at wholesale. He proudly hung a sign outside his store with the words, "Singer Sewing Machines" and his name as agent. It was a simple agreement, and very profitable for ambitious, hardworking agents, many of whom amassed small fortunes. Following Singer came companies like Watkins and Rawleighs (household and farm products sold house to house). Later, gasoline, automobiles, and other products were sold by franchise.

Value to the Franchisor

The value to franchisors is that franchise arrangements provide additional outlets for their product or services, usually without any out-of-pocket expense or gamble.

The value to the franchisee is that the amateur merchant immediately acquires the expertise of the professional merchant, and frequently makes money right from the beginning. When you figure that at least eight of ten independent businesses go under, it could be well worth purchasing a franchise and operating on their know-how. They'll usually have experts to get you started, and check with you regularly. They will show you how to prepare, display, and merchandise their product. In fact, most franchisors want the new operator to spend some time at head office before starting out.

Facts on Franchising

If you are "accepted" by a franchise house they will probably tell you how to raise any needed capital. Many new operators mortgage their homes, borrow on life insurance, go to their bank, and sometimes borrow from relatives or friends. Obviously it will depend on the franchise you get, as to how much capital you'll require. The cost can run from a thousand dollars to one hundred thousand dollars or more. This depends on whether you are going to rent a place of operation and build a franchise outlet, or whether it is going to be a small, home operation, handled in spare hours. Many professional people find it profitable to operate a franchise — particularly food — and hire employees to run the business for them.

Most franchisors have rigid regulations about how close franchisees can be located to their nearest outlet, and also facts on the competition. It is reported that in Canada and the United States there are about one million franchises and there are now many in Europe and the Far East. They are also springing up in many Caribbean and South Pacific Islands.

While sales increases in independent businesses average five percent a year, the franchise outlets show an increase of at least ten percent.

What is your Cost?

If you are going to buy a retail franchise, you can expect to pay a percentage averaging from four to eight percent of sales to the franchisor. Your costs, in addition to a percentage of sales, usually include a charge for the company sign, any equipment used in the business, staff training, product purchase, uniforms, advertising, and the cost of any building and parking area.

There is often an additional charge for what is known as cluster advertising. If for example there are a number of the same outlets in one territory you may expect to be charged for an advertising campaign which would run specials applying only to your area. The product or service may be promoted rather than the name or address of any particular franchisee.

It is estimated that there are eleven hundred companies offering franchises in Canada and the United States (for example, McDonald's, Baskins & Robbins, and Colonel Sander's Kentucky Fried Chicken). An important factor in the increase in food establishment franchises has been the introduction of seating service. Originally most food outlets were "at the counter" types.

Help in Finding the Right Location

In the event that you make a deal and you have to find a location, the franchisor will likely conduct a survey. This will include pedestrian and traffic reports, to be sure you have a location that will pay off. The competition will also be considered. There is one firm that likes to locate very close to a competitor, because they feel that their prices and quality will take customers away from their competition.

Franchisors say that most outlets succeed. If they don't, it is generally because the operator has not followed company policy, and has attempted to introduce his or her own variations. Said one franchisor, "We spend months or maybe years working out everything to the last detail, even to how many drops of ketchup on a hamburger, and an amateur comes along and tries to improve on our methods."

A hotel man with a small place (fifty rooms) in Northern Ontario, said he joined the Sheraton group ten years ago and is delighted he did. The system (referrals) whereby guests book in advance, has doubled his business. Also the money he saves in buying linen and other products is very substantial.

Franchise Operations Spread

While many franchisors operate from plush office buildings which they often own, and have dozens of well-trained executives criss-crossing the country, checking on service, there are also one-person franchisors. These people often capitalize on the franchise trend.

They may manufacture, or represent, such items as cosmetics, health foods, and various other products. They will come into an area, run enticing classified ads offering exclusive representation, without asking for a joining fee. What they are offering is an instruction booklet, plus a certain quantity of their products for a certain price. This could be as low as five hundred dollars. After the buyer's basement has been loaded with their products, the operator is off to the next call, and the franchisee is wondering what to do with this great "treasure" of unknown products. The buyer, without the support from the franchisor, can only run a few classified ads in the hope of getting sales people, or hold house parties with a view to getting rid of the product.

Franchise associations say that before investing it pays to investigate. Ask to see the franchisor's financial statements. Find out how many franchises they have. If possible contact one of their franchise outlets and ask whether they are happy with the service, the product, profit, and anything else that will enable you to make an educated/knowledgable decision.

The Man of Eighty-six

I met an eighty-six-year-old man in Maine, who had only recently retired. He owned and operated his own franchise business, selling courses showing the benefits of health foods. He advertised in food and health journals. His ads invited people to send for free information on how to start and operate a profitable health food store.

Those who wrote for information received a four-page folder, a coupon, and a return envelope. This package described the three hundred dollar ten lesson course he offered. Inquiries came in daily, and so did the three hundred dollar cheques. This man operated out of a farm house and said that he had customers from California and Vancouver!

Each of his ten lessons included a booklet which was twenty pages long. He had invested in a plastic binding machine so that the booklets, with their plastic bound covers, looked very professional. He figured there was enough information in the course to open a store, and that the stores he "had inspired" dotted the country.

Hamburgers and Chicken Most Popular

While the most popular franchises are fast-food chains: hamburger, chicken, fish, pizza, submarine sandwiches, and doughnuts; there are many other franchise products and services available. A few are printing, dry cleaning, maid service, employment agencies, clothing, music, travel, real estate, nursing homes, accounting, tax services, car rentals and sales, gas stations, convenience stores, art, soft drinks, cosmetics, schools of all types, dance and reducing studios.

One of the main benefits to individual operators is advertising. Today, if you don't advertise, you might as well give up. A franchisor with many outlets can dominate the market, yet the cost to the individual franchisee can be very low.

Start on Your Own?

The advantages of joining with a successful franchisor are many. It has, after all, opened dozens, or maybe hundreds, of outlets. It is to the franchisor's advantage to get and keep you profitable. You can benefit from the franchisor's experience all down the line. On the other hand this know-how can be costly. Many people have taken a job in a franchise outlet to get an idea how the business is operated, before going out on their own.

One twenty-seven-year-old man started a submarine sandwich and pizza shop, after gaining some experience in the business. He rented a store, put in an oven and counter, and made arrangements with suppliers. He would have had to do this anyway on a franchise deal and it would have cost much more. Now he could keep costs down, and be his own boss. After six months he has a staff of five and is open from 11 a.m. to 11 p.m. He offers fast delivery and is doing very well. He says fresh ingredients are the keystone of success. His hot roast beef submarine sandwich sells for three dollars and seventy-five cents, with all the trimmings. He put out circulars around the area when he first opened, offering a discount coupon worth a dollar on any item. The customers were lined up. His second outlet will be opening shortly. So it may pay you to consider starting on your own!

Further Information

For further details contact Canadian Franchising Association, 150 Eglington Avenue West, Toronto, Ontario, M4P IE8, or phone (416)483-6106. They represent all major franchisors in Canada. In the United States there is the International Franchisors Association, 1350 New York Avenue, Washington, D.C., or phone (202)628-8000.

For a copy of the 1986 Franchise Annual, listing all franchises in Canada, send $19.95 to Info Press, 11 Bond Street, St. Catharines, Ontario, L2R 4Z4, (416)688-2665. The Federal Business Development Bank, Ottawa, Ontario also has many helpful folders available on small business operations. There is a booklet entitled "Facts about Franchising" available from the Ministry of Consumer and Commercial Relations, 555 Yonge Street, Toronto, Ontario, M6A 2H6.

11
Start Your Own Periodical Without Money!

Have you ever thought of owning your own little periodical? If you are really serious about it, a periodical can be a great spare-time business that might become a full-time, profitable business. Very often a periodical can be started with very little capital.

Basically there are three different types of periodicals, so let us look at each one. This may give you some perspective on what it's all about.

The Trade Magazine

There are about three hundred business magazines (trade journals) in Canada, and at least ten times this number in the United States. They come under such titles as *Canadian Grocer*, and *American Dry Cleaner*. To get a complete list of trade periodicals in Canada, see Canadian Advertising, Rates and Data, Maclean Hunter, 777 Bay Street, Toronto, Ontario, M5W 1A7, or in the United States, Standard Rate and Data Service Inc., 3004 Glenview Road, Wilmette, IL 60091.

If you are in touch with an ad agency, they may loan you issues of one of these periodicals, or you can check with your library for directories. These directories are expensive. They run from thirty-five to a hundred dollars a copy, and libraries regard them as reference books, which means they cannot be taken out.

Trade magazines were started in Canada over a hundred years ago, and probably just as early elsewhere in the world. Their main reason for being, in those early days, was to advise wholesale and retail merchants about what goods were available. This included shipments of goods that arrived from overseas, and those manufactured on the home market. This information was most important to the trade. For instance, a news item in a grocery magazine might have read, "Arriving from Hong Kong by the *S.S. Espanola*, ten thousand pounds of black tea in one hundred pound crates. Date of delivery is expected to be early July, 1849."

Of prime interest to retailers was the name of the wholesaler of this and other products. As a result, magazine owners would contact wholesalers to run ads containing specific information about what merchandise they had available. In those days a retailer, known as a general merchant, sold just about everything and could get his information from just one magazine. But, as the population increased and departments became larger, there was a fragmentation in retailing and other businesses. Instead of being under one roof, there appeared separate hardware stores, grocery stores, clothing stores, and so on. The last magazine serving Canadian general merchants, General Merchant of Canada (Maclean Hunter) ended publication in the mid-1940s after almost a century of service.

New Opportunities

Almost every business field from retailing to wholesaling to manufacturing is represented by one or more publications. Still there are always opportunities for another, and this is proven by the fact that new ones start every year.

If you are thinking about publishing a magazine for a specific trade, you must study all aspects of it. Make yourself an authority on the subject. General information will do for an overall picture, but more specific knowledge is necessary in the particular field in which you are interested.

How Can You Buy An Existing Trade Magazine?

A bakery magazine was ready to close down because the publisher had other, more profitable interests. This magazine wasn't selling more than three or four hundred dollars an issue in advertising. But it did have subscribers; about four thousand of them. And, by law, should a publisher decide, for whatever reason — apart from bankruptcy — to cease publication of the magazine, he is responsible for refunding the total subscriber debt. Subscriber debt is the term used to refer to the total amount of money or issues outstanding in a prepaid subscription.

Consequently, magazines of all types can often be picked up cheaply, as the new publisher is expected to continue to service all subscribers, thus letting the old publisher off the hook. Sometimes publishers will pay to have someone take over a magazine faced with problems. I paid no more than five hundred dollars for the bakery magazine I mentioned, and, after building up its advertising, had no difficulty selling it for sixty-five thousand dollars. I understand it is still doing very well today.

Actually, a publisher, while he or she may pay a large sum for a magazine, often operates this way. They will make a small down payment and the balance is paid on the basis of a ten percent royalty of the advertising gross annually, or ten percent of renewal subscriptions, or a combination of both. As most new publishers increase circulation quickly, they can raise their advertising rates by at least ten percent thus, they are really paying very little for the new magazine.

Getting Started

You can contact publishers asking if they have anything available, although you may get offers at outrageous figures. But somewhere, sometime, you might just get a response that excites you. Also, if you check through ad directories, you might notice a subject that doesn't seem to be represented. This could be where one publisher has joined two similar papers leaving a void for the small operator to fill.

The most inexpensive way of starting a trade magazine with little money is to print a circular. No more than five hundred, one-sided folders are usually enough. You would then send these circulars to advertising prospects. There are directories listing suppliers in every business. Once again, check with your library.

Your circular can be typed, photocopied and should carry the name of your proposed publication. Once again, you can check directories to see that there is no similar name. The circular you send out should mention your total expected circulation, i.e. wholesalers, retailers, manufacturers, plus your ad rates. Don't forget your subscription rates. New trade papers are usually mailed free to readers; this is called controlled circulation. Thus a circular might read, "Controlled circulation guarantees a distribution of twenty-five hundred."

If your idea is a good one and your circular looks professional, you could get an eager response. Once you start, keep your costs as low as possible. If you are anxious enough, and spend every spare minute pushing your baby, you could end up with a healthy offspring that could keep you in your old age.

12
Starting a Small Newspaper

As you may have noticed if you live on the outskirts of a city, the local daily keeps expanding its circulation, resulting in the blanketing of a large area. This, of course, has generally meant that there is less specific area news being published. While a city paper's circulation might grow, the number of pages per issue may remain the same, or even decrease.

Moreover, outlying areas have become more heavily populated, and the number of retail establishments has increased. These local merchants are usually not keen about advertising in the big city daily because they are paying for distribution that won't bring in customers.

Low Area Rates

Therefore many small weeklies have sprung up which serve one or two small areas only. At the moment, there are over eight hundred weekly papers in Canada and about eight thousand in the United States.

To start a weekly you should set your own type. You can use a typewriter, or rent a professional typesetting machine. Next, make up a "dummy" (a facsimile of what your first issue will look like) — tabloid size is best — and call on local merchants and offer them advertising space. Once again, check with directories to get an idea what weeklies around the country are charging for ads and what kind of circulation they have. You may want to "drop" the first few issues at area homes until the subscriptions start to roll in. Also contact printers willing to print from your camera-ready pages. If you put out a twelve-page paper with one thousand circulation at the beginning, your print costs should be very low. It is wise to run half advertising and half editorial.

A small weekly can be produced in spare hours, and you might be surprised how much advertising you'll get. Associations and churches will supply you with a lot of your news. A good part-time editorial person will prove invaluable. You might also get columnists who will work for by-lines.

As stated in the previous chapter on publishing, do your best to keep costs down!

13
Starting a Consumer (Hobby) Magazine

If you are interested in starting a magazine with little or no money, then, of course, you can't consider anything that sells on newsstands at a national level. However, a few local outlets might be interested in handling your publication on a one-third commission basis.

A hobby magazine is the easiest type of small paper to handle. It can come out monthly, or even quarterly (four times a year). Subscriptions are important for your cash flow, and these can be gotten from club members and associations of the type your magazine caters to. You might attend local meetings or give free issues in order to pick up subscriptions. You can also run classified subscription ads in papers similar to yours.

Of course you should set your own type and give ready-to-print material to your printer. This will save money. Also, go to a copy centre for fast work and low prices. Surveys are important to find out if there is a need for the hobby publication you have in mind. As you will have few, if any, large ads, your paper won't have to be glossy in appearance.

Contact your main post office and arrange to get magazine postal rates. Only the main postal office in your region can get you a publisher's rate mailing permit. You may have to mail your first issue or two at regular rates before your publication is approved for special mailing privileges.

A hobby magazine could fill a real need and can often be profitable and exciting.

14
Publicity Can Make Sales for You

Publicity can be free. It is the greatest thing imaginable for the small business person or, for that matter, any business. Big businesses often employ a large staff to work on publicity. Other firms employ public relations (PR) companies to get publicity for them, spending big money in the process. Companies also spend money to keep their name *out* of the paper if something unfavourable happens.

There are six thousand restaurants in Chicago and about twenty full-time critics who work for radio, TV and newspapers giving reports on new and established restaurants in the city. It is estimated that fifteen restaurants open daily in this city but that only some get reviewed. Critics, it is reported, use all sorts of disguises from dark glasses to false noses so they won't be recognized.

Apparently a bad review can drive a new restaurant out of business, while a good review can turn a new restaurant into a success. Some restaurants which have received bad reviews often take large ad space to explain why things are not as bad as they are painted. Although one established restaurant reported that a poor review reduced business by about only ten percent, and that most old-time customers continued to patronize the place.

How to Get Publicity

The reason good publicity is so desirable is that it attracts attention and it's often free. Press releases are more likely to influence newspaper and magazine readers — as well as radio listeners — than ads do, and, to the business person, this method of getting publicity is extremely exciting.

For example, I wrote a booklet on photography and sent a copy to a photography magazine published by Maclean Hunter. The editor of that paper reviewed it. He said in part, "It has plenty of ideas for the amateur who wants to make money in photography." The rest wasn't as flattering, as he criticized the printing, but he mentioned the price of five dollars and my address. What more could you ask? His magazine had hardly hit the newsstands before the orders came pouring in. And that's the way it is. You send out a sample of your product with a brief release mentioning the price and your address, and anything can happen.

Magazine and newspaper editors are looking for news; that is their job. When they get your material, particularly if there is a photograph of the product, you are halfway to heaven. Radio stations like this material too. TV is much harder to influence. Newspapers are only fair as they have a very short life. Magazines are best. Many of them, both trade and consumer, run columns under the general title "What's New?"

What's New?

If there is a new angle to your product or service, then that may be the dominant factor in obtaining publicity. If it is a product sold by retailers then the prime source of publicity should be magazines of the type the dealer would read. For example, a new grocery package or product would be of interest to editors of grocery magazines. It might also be of interest to women's magazines, and the women's section of daily newspapers.

Give It An Angle

Having an angle is important. If your angle is exciting enough it may also be of interest to radio and TV stations. One PR man got tremendous publicity because he said his client's pen wrote under water. The public were not interested in writing under water, but the idea of owning one which could interested them. So, when they wanted to buy a pen they asked to see the one which wrote under water.

Sometimes, publicity comes in a strange way. Two young women were once adrift for many days on the South Pacific Ocean, and all they had to eat was Colgate toothpaste. All the media in the land mentioned it. If Colgate were to buy this much publicity, it would have cost a million dollars, or more. The people at Colgate were so pleased by the exposure that they sent the girls enough toothpaste for years. This got additional PR for the company.

The Short Article that Paid Off

A young newspaper man in California got a press release from Washington, saying that there were people around who were passing counterfeit twenty-dollar bills. This man worked for a weekly newspaper. He used the story, and also ran the picture that came with the release, which showed how to detect fake twenties.

He began wondering how many editors read this government release and used it, in view of the fact that hundreds of releases arrive every day on editors' desks.

This man was also a freelance writer. He reasoned that because he was paying taxes, he had indirectly paid for at least part of the release. He had a few hundred copies made of the photo of the fake twenty, and rewrote the release. If Washington wanted publicity, he would get it for them. He photocopied his own release which he figured was brighter than the government handout and sent it off to a few hundred newspapers. (There are about eighteen hundred daily newspapers in the United States and one hundred in Canada.)

Sure, he was gambling time and money — but the results were phenomenal. He had put the words "Freelance Writer" on the one-page sheet containing his story so that editors would not think it was a free release.

He reports that some big papers paid him as much as fifty dollars for the story, and smaller papers as little as ten dollars. But when he figured it out, he had cleared about five thousand dollars for something on which he had spent no more than ten days of his spare time.

When this was over, he decided that trade paper editors might be interested too. So he sent out a release and photograph to editors putting out retail trade papers. He made slight changes to the first few words of each story to appeal to the different readers. For example, the sort going to jewellery magazines read, "Jewellers can avoid being gypped out of twenty-dollar bills by . . . ," and to hardware readers, "Hardware people can avoid being gypped out of twenty-dollar bills by . . . ," and so forth. Sales were heavy here too.

Incidentally, newspapers normally buy items on a non-exclusive basis, so an item or story can be sent to many papers, but it's not a good idea to send it to two papers in the same city.

Promoting Your Own Product

If you have a product or service that you feel is unusual enough to attract editorial attention, send out samples and a press release. If you advertise in a particular publication, then publicity could be easier to get in that paper.

If you ever advertise on radio, you may ask to voice the commercial, as this gives it more credibility. So, if you have what is called a radio voice, investigate this option. While you pay for this "time" it provides good PR. These days, radio has more listeners than ever.

An American PR firm now offers a service to book publishers who want to expose their authors on various talk shows. This PR firm says that many writers do their book more harm than good and, for a fee, this company will train writers how to speak in front of a mike. Some writers may not have read their book for some time and reviewers may ask them critical questions about it. Some phone-in listeners may put the writer on the spot with embarrassing questions. These are some of the problems this agency will help the author clear up, as well as showing them how to speak clearly and slowly. One phone-in person asked an author what language he was speaking because he couldn't understand him. Certain talk shows both in Canada and the United States are apparently more favourably disposed to guests who are trained by this agency.

So before contacting a radio or TV station, make sure you are "ready to go on."

15
Your Camera Can Become A Money-Making Machine

If you have any interest at all in photography, you can make money at it. You can do this in spare hours and operate right from your home.

I have made money over the years with my camera. Usually I use a relatively inexpensive camera, traded in when a better model appears. Right now I have a 35 mm S.F. camera. The S.F. means self-focusing. You just aim the camera at the subject or object you want, push a button for the automatic flash to come into position (if you decide the scene needs brightening up) and shoot the picture!

I don't bother with special equipment such as wide angle lenses, flood lights, and meters. I leave this to the professional photographer who usually gets a better picture but at ten times what I am paid. But I fill a need. He won't shoot what I shoot, and I certainly can't shoot what he shoots.

Let the Camera be the Judge

The professional photographer is master of his or her equipment, and will know what type of equipment they need to get the required picture. The professional is also required to take all types of photos, including packages of soft drinks, models, cars, new styles, furniture, and so forth. He also does a lot of "touching up" in the darkroom, removing shadows, brightening up negatives and so on. Most professionals spend a small fortune on their equipment.

I send my rolls of film to a camera shop or drug store for processing. Most places send their work to photo-finishing labs, all of whom use about the same expensive, automatic processing equipment.

With my camera I got an instruction booklet. If you buy a new camera you'll get one too. Study it, and you will learn what the camera is capable of. That's where the pro and amateurs like me differ. The pro buys equipment that will enable him to handle any job that comes along. The amateur lets his camera decide what type of photos can be shot, and then shoots specific pictures; nothing too elaborate, no ad shots, no involved pictures, or techniques.

First, you should always shoot in colour. In the old days colour was a luxury. Now colour film and processing are cheaper than black and white.

Here are some of the standard items you can shoot for money. Visit a shopping centre; wander through the stores — particularly the independents. If you see an interesting display, ask the manager if he'd like a shot of it. He may want to keep a picture for next year, to see what he did this year. You have your camera along and you shoot right away. No fuss, no problems. In order to have a professional shoot the picture, the store manager would have to make an appointment, maybe order a half-dozen 8" x 10"s at a cost that could be as high as a hundred dollars.

But you'll give him pix at around fifteen dollars. Your photo finisher will probably give you post card size prints. Now you may have the manager and his staff pose for additional shots and sell these photos to them at a few dollars each. You might also pick up an additional sale or two by sending a photo and cutline to a men's clothing journal. There are many types of stores worth contacting for this kind of business.

However, I discovered that instant-type photo cameras weren't suitable for this kind of work, as film costs were higher than roll negatives, and as no negative exists, there is no reprint business — which can be substantial.

Special Celebration

Let's say a small company is holding a party — you can usually get the okay to wander around and shoot pictures. I've never bothered with the names of people whose pictures I've taken. I would just deliver my pix to someone in the office, maybe a friend. I would agree to see him in a couple of days. I would have placed a number on the back of each picture. When I returned he would usually give me a list of prints wanted. This might read: No. 5 — ten copies; No. 2 — five copies, etc. At three dollars a print, fifty dollars in total for two hours of work was not unusual.

Golf is Good, too

If a company is holding its annual golf game — and there are many who do this — you can make good money. Shoot people teeing off, putting, receiving prizes at the evening banquet. Appoint someone to get orders and cash from your set of samples. This can all be done in a week or so. Companies usually prefer this as they don't have to offer any guarantees, or photo commitments of any kind.

Also worthwhile are bowling games, card games, amateur sports events, anniversary parties, receptions, and so forth. You'll be surprised how profitable such a business can be in a short time, and you can start with the inexpensive camera you now have. It'll only take a little practice in framing before shooting.

Remember, if you want people in the picture to be recognizable, shoot the picture close up. There is no need to include the lower part of their body in the shot unless, for example, they are putting on a golf green. Action pictures are best. Get your subject doing something — something natural. For example, I was asked to take a picture of people standing by a yacht. They all lined up like soldiers. I could imagine how wooden the picture would look, so I had them relax. I placed them around the boat in sitting or working positions. A fellow at the wheel, two or three women sprawled at the front of the deck, and a couple on deck chairs. The picture looked natural, and sales were excellent. Think about how your scene will look (framing) before you shoot. Regard your shot the way an artist looks at a proposed picture. This framing applies to any picture.

Try an experiment — try to get an exciting shot of a fisherman. Tie a stone at the end of his fishing line. Tell him or her to look intently at the end of the line, maybe even holding the net. Action is interest.

Sometimes pictures can be sold to weekly or daily papers. Also, check with small independent stores. Their trade journals are always interested in unusual pictures, and pay ten to twenty-five dollars for a post card size print. They prefer colour, so that they can run it in colour or black and white, as they wish. A detailed cutline (description) is necessary. This includes name and address of store, owner, and facts about the picture.

Here are a few pictures I have sold: a sign shaped like a mammoth saw outside a hardware store; a 1925 model car atop a garage, advertising repair services; a group of dummy models in a clothing store; stuffed ducks in a sports store window; mannequins in a women's store, advertising latest fashions.

Store windows should be shot at night to eliminate glare. Window lights must be on, so you will not need to use a flash. These pictures can be time-shots, with the lens open at a small aperture, for three or four seconds. This requires practice, and a tripod.

Attractive interior store displays are also in demand. Just recently I sold ten different photos of a renovated hardware store to a trade journal. This netted two hundred and fifty dollars for the pix and details.

There is little competition for the ambitious freelancer who keeps an eye open for salable pixs and keeps trying to sell his work through the mail.

16
The Wealthy Shoemaker

Businesses advertised under "Business for Sale" are often bargains, and they can be very profitable. Let me give you an example. A fellow was working in Seven Islands, Quebec, when he was laid off. One day, while he was out, his garage and car caught fire. After collecting compensation from the insurance company, he moved to a larger city, where he saw an ad for a business for sale.

The ad had been placed by a shopping centre whose tenant had gone bankrupt and the business was a dry cleaning establishment. The previous owner had been making seven hundred dollars a week, which was not enough to pay the monthly rent as well as a percentage of sales, which most shopping centres charge. Then there were wages for washer and dryer operators, and a repair person. It was the owner's job to handle the orders.

The man from Seven Islands was offered the store and equipment, in exchange for the rent owed by the previous tenant. The new man knew nothing about dry cleaning, but fortunately there was a woman who had worked at the place for two years and knew every operation. He brought her back, and he also contacted the washer/dryer sales agent, who gave the new owner many tips. He would be buying cleaning solvents regularly so would be a good customer for the agent. He might also be in the market for new equipment to replace the well-used products he had, so it was to the agent's advantage to give him all the help he could.

The shopping centre was pleased to sell everything as part of the rent balance. There is nothing worse in a shopping centre than an empty store.

The Owner Expands his Business

Soon after this man got going, people began asking him if he knew of a good place for shoe repairs. In fact, there had been eight children in his father's family, and the boys had been expected to help with shoe repairs. So, since he knew something about repairing shoes, he purchased the appropriate equipment and offered a shoe repair service.

Before long a commercial washer and dryer came up for sale and he was also able to obtain these units. Soon he had increased his staff, and within a year sales were up to five thousand dollars a week. He says it took him about two years to go from his little house on the north shore of the St. Lawrence River to a position where he was clearing thirty-five thousand dollars a year. Although he admits it is a lot of hard work and responsibility, he says, "It's great being your own boss, and making money too."

17
Be a Printing Jobber

This is a type of business which is popular in many areas, and offers excellent part-time opportunities. You don't have to be an expert in printing to start, but some knowledge of the business is preferable.

Here is how most operators work. They contact likely prospects and pick up orders for business cards, envelopes, letterheads, circulars, statements, and invoices. A sales person often deals with printers who specialize in the kind of work for which he or she gets orders — for example, business cards are usually handled by firms specializing in this item. Circulars may be done by another company. A representative may deal with a half-dozen houses, and will have the work done by the house that gives the best price, quality, and service for each particular job.

Printing jobbers may do their own invoicing, adding their commission to the wholesale price. Added to this, there could be charges for writing copy, art work, layout, proofing, and so on. Customers often need other work, so this can build into a good business.

18
Money in Bookbinding

Bookbinding has been popular for years, often as a part-time money-making hobby, but now a new aspect has been added. I know of a retired gentleman who has been binding worn books for some time, but a year ago he discovered that there was also a need for someone to repair old sheet music.

This happened when a church called him and said that much of their old sheet music was in very poor condition. They thought that their music, used by forty members of the choir, was irreplaceable, since much of it was no longer available. Its value was estimated at ten thousand dollars.

The bookbinder agreed to repair all their worn sheet music for a fee of one thousand dollars, which the church was happy to pay.

This man made photocopies of much of the work and put it all together in solid condition much to the delight of the choir and other church members. He also got the contract to repair worn and torn hymnals and other works.

This fellow reports that libraries and book retailers who specialize in rare books are also good customers. Simple and inexpensive courses in bookbinding are widely available through your local educational institutions.

19
Private MailBox Service

A woman in California is making history. It seems she wanted to get her mail by post office box, but wanted it anytime . . . all day Saturday, Sundays, and holidays. She felt other people might feel the same way, so she took a small store and offered a mailbox service, where, for a charge, people could rent a box and pick up their mail almost any time. They could also have the mailbox operator readdress and forward mail if they were away on holiday. There was an additional charge for this service.

This business grew and she found she was having difficulty getting all the metal mailboxes she needed. So, with her profits she started manufacturing mailboxes for her own post office.

Apparently the United States government had difficulty getting all the boxes *they* required, so they gave her their orders, too. Today, she has a big mailbox manufacturing business going, as well as her personal mailbox service.

20
A Convenience Store

The corner grocery has become a convenience store, and generally carries a large stock and stays open long hours. In fact, some of them never close.

There are three types of convenience stores. There are chain operators, franchise stores, and complete independents. Prices are high compared to supermarkets because these stores offer convenience shopping rather than supermarket bargains. Many are operated by people who have other jobs, and depend on managers, staff, or even family members to do the work.

Whichever of the three types of operation is chosen, operators have to make a profit if they are to stay in business. If it's a franchise or manager/percentage deal, the operator will be responsible for any stock losses. Head office will take stock regularly and the manager is expected to make good on any shortages.

Which is the Best Deal?

If you take over a franchise or go in as a manager of a chain you won't have to worry about finding a location, although you will have to make an investment in a franchise operation. However, a job with a going convenience store is excellent training if you intend to start your own business.

Location is extremely important, and an attractive store in a good location can be half the battle, if you know the business. Because you will not be buying in supermarket quantities your wholesale price may be a penny or two higher than your big competition, but your "open all hours" policy will enable you to charge a little more.

Because wholesalers will realize that you are a good source of revenue for them, many will give you good credit terms, and because of the type of store you are running, you can buy often and in small lots. Pleasant store personnel are essential, and relatives and family members can be a great help.

21
Be a "Garage Sale" Manager

It had to come. Now there are managers of garage sales, and you could train yourself to be one. Here's how it works.

If you intend to hold a garage sale, there are ambitious people who will attend to all the details for you. They will probably make more money for you, and a percentage for themselves.

On the other hand, if you wish to become an operator of this type of business, here is what you do. Watch for announcements of coming garage sales, or contact people that you hear are going to hold such a sale. Suggest a partnership. It will be your job to place all items in the driveway or garage, price them, and handle all sales and collect the payment. Because you'll probably be a stranger to most "shoppers," you won't feel embarrassed about having to haggle.

Many people using outside help report high total sales. On a twenty-five percent profit basis, operators can do well, especially if they can get eight sales a month.

Operators can advertise with such catchy little ads as "Let us handle your next garage sale! We do all the work and charge only a percentage of sales."

22
Book Remainders Can be Profitable

Selling books by mail or to clubs can be a profitable spare-time business, if handled properly. Books that publishers have left over — such as overruns — are sometimes sold at reduced prices to agents who specialize in this business.

A good example might be a travel book. It has done reasonably well on the market, but the publisher has a new travel book coming out. This could be a ten dollar (retail) book available at a dollar or so a copy; as is, with no returns. There are agents who buy these books in quantity and offer them as "remainders." An agent will charge a dollar more than he paid for them, if you buy in small quantities.

I once bought five hundred books from an agent at a dollar a copy. They were about memory-training. I offered them at five dollars each, and sold out. I advertised them in a magazine I published.

If you send a request about "remainders" to a number of publishers, you could get some interesting answers. Fiction is a poor seller for this method, as your outlets are limited. But specialized non-fiction can be successful. For instance, if you have a camera book, contact photo clubs in different cities by circular. The local camera club will tell you the names of other clubs. Members often buy these reduced items if they are of interest and a genuine bargain.

Classified ads in photo journals could pay off, too. Other hobby books are worth considering, such as stamps, coins, needlecraft, cooking, among others.

23
Odd Jobs

A man had worked in the office of a large manufacturer, in the payroll department, for over ten years. But he hated every moment of it. A friend had gotten him in when it was difficult to find work, and he was still there at age thirty-seven. He lived in a town of five thousand people, most of whom owned their own home. He kept telling himself that he had security.

He Put Spare Hours to Work

This man was handy with tools. He always did repairs around the house, which he enjoyed. So he let it be known that he was available for home repairs. His rate was sixteen dollars an hour. He did roof repairs, painting, landscaping, carpentry, and snow removal when he was available. He had a station wagon which he used to transport his snowblower, lawnmower, and various other tools.

He was doing this work in his spare hours, but hired a young fellow to do the work during the week. Soon the new orders, repeats, and referrals — all without any advertising — became so heavy he decided to quit his job.

He admits he wasn't an expert in many of the jobs he was called on to do, but he learned quickly and always arrived at a job when he said he would. He continued for over a year with his standard price — sixteen dollars an hour — but raised it a little the second year.

If the job comes to less than an hour, he charges accordingly. The cost of any supplies are additional. He made a deal with the local hardware store to buy all his needs there and they offered him a twenty percent discount. He had business cards printed, and the hardware store hands them out to likely prospects. This works out very well, and helps the handyman.

One of his big money-makers in winter is snow removal. He has a number of stores and residential customers. He signs agreements with clients in the fall and quotes them a price for the entire winter. The price is usually one hundred (private homes) to five hundred (businesses) dollars for driveways and sidewalks. He may start work at three in the morning if there has been a heavy snowfall the night before.

He says this business pays very well, and he is only sorry he didn't start it earlier.

24
Video Tape to the Rescue

A relatively new business is taking movies of people's possessions. In the event of damage or loss, people can show insurance firms actual films of what they lost. You approach a prospect and suggest a movie be taken of every room in their house, as well as close-up shots of radios, stereos, jewellery, silver, collections, and any other expensive articles. Drawers should be opened and filmed so that storage conditions can be shown. The video tape is left with the client, to be stored in a safety deposit box at the bank for safe-keeping. There should be no other copies of the film.

Tape the Reading of a Will

Some people also have their wills videotaped. A photographer will make a movie of the client reading a will, designating who gets what. After the client has died, the family gathers around the TV and plays the video tape and if properly done, there is no doubt that the client can better explain *exactly* how he wants to dispose of his or her assets. In certain areas of North America a video is considered a legal document, whereas in others a written will is also necessary. Contact a lawyer to determine the validity of videos in any given area.

25
Complete Lawn Service

A great part-time money-maker is the provision of complete lawn service. Some people require this because their schedule is full during the day, and they cannot find the time to do the work themselves. They could also have allergies and be unable to work around grass or plants. Seniors and physically impaired people also require help with heavy seasonal planting, trimming and raking, and are grateful for this service when it is available.

However, if you sign a contract, honour it. It is necessary to supply regular service. It's possible to hire students to do much or all of the work while you look after the business end, taking orders, making sure your staff are on the job, inspecting work done, and making collections. Your services could include grass-cutting, hedge-trimming, weeding, snow removal, and other lawn services.

26
Knitting Machines Are Money-Makers

A woman who retired from office work decided to go in for knitting to help pass the time and make extra money. She contacted a department store and found that automatic knitting machines cost five hundred to twelve hundred dollars. She wanted an additional unit called a ribber for the fine finishing of sweaters. This was an extra three hundred dollars. Her total purchase amounted to eight hundred dollars.

She studied all the directions carefully. Someone at the store told her that knitting machines had only been on the market for a few years and had improved considerably during that time. She learned that she could change a pattern in five minutes, and produce a wool sweater automatically in four hours.

She took a couple of sample sweaters and some baby layettes to her former office, where the employees said, "You cannot tell the work from the handknitted variety."

She charged sixty dollars each for the average ladies' or man's sweater, and found she could produce two a day without any difficulty. During the first month of operation she got orders for two dozen sweaters from her old office, with promises of more for holiday gifts. She says sometimes people want intricate designs and styles that require hand-knitting, but she can turn out most orders on the machine and make a good profit. When she delivers a sweater she frequently gets orders from the customer's friends. In addition to sweaters, leg warmers for dancers are a popular item, and simple to make on this machine. Post a sign advertising your business in all your local ballet schools, and where aerobic classes are offered.

27
Hand Knitting Still in Demand

I know of a woman who works in an office on the switchboard and, in her spare moments, knits sweaters. She charges an average of fifty dollars a sweater, but customers supply their own wool, and also the patterns.

Hand knitted sweaters and other knitted goods usually bring somewhat more than machine-produced products. Very popular are baby items such as booties, socks, little sweaters, and suits. They make excellent gifts.

Sell to Boutiques

If you get a real operation going you might want to place some of your work with boutiques and various speciality shops. Merchants usually ask for at least one-third off retail. You might raise your prices slightly to what you have been charging personal customers.

28
Newsletters are Worthwhile

You don't have to be an experienced writer to turn out a newsletter. This is probably the simplest form of journalism, yet it can be very profitable.

First you choose a topic you know something about. This could be a hobby, your work, or some other subject that appeals to you. It doesn't matter if there are already newsletters on the subject you have chosen. With the hundreds of newsletters already available, it would be very difficult to pick one which was exclusive in its field. There are newsletters about antiques, automobiles, finance, stocks, business, clothes, child care, photography, gardening, and many other subjects.

Getting Information

Say your interest is photography. You would have an inexpensive letterhead done by a copy shop. You could call it "Monthly Photo News" for example. Then you would write to the head offices of as many camera firms as you could find. Tell them you are publishing a newsletter and you would like to be put on their mailing list for releases. Before long you will be deluged with news releases, which would cover special bargains, new products, etc. You could try any business you wish, the results would be the same.

You could also develop other sources of news, such as photofinishing, markets for photos, and reviews of new books on photography (books for review purposes are free from publishers). Running stories about well-known photographers and the various interesting trips photographers might take to find good photos and other news. You would be writing for amateurs like yourself.

Newsletters are printed on both sides of an 8½ x 11 inch sheet, and run to three or four sheets. That's about maximum for a first-class letter, the postal method used by most newsletter publishers.

Getting Subscribers

After typing out your news, you would give the finished job to your copy centre to print from. The newsletter shouldn't cost more than twenty-five cents a copy to print. You can put out your letter as frequently as you wish. Prices of newsletters vary from ten dollars a year (coming out every second month) to two hundred dollars a year (for a daily letter).

Your big job is to get subscribers. For instance, if you decided on a photography newsletter, you could visit camera clubs and tell them about it. You could give special offers to anyone subscribing for two years. You might also run classified ads in photo magazines, and send out press releases.

The main difference between a newsletter and a magazine is that a newsletter can be mailed first class in a no. 10 envelope because it has so few pages. Unlike magazines, newsletters don't carry advertising. Newsletter publishing is a great spare-time business. It does not take much money to get started and you will be surprised how easily the subscriptions come in.

29
Rent a Section of a Large Store

I noted with interest, particularly while travelling through the United States, that a number of larger stores rent out small sections. This makes a lot of sense to both the store and the tenant. Let's say a store sells many lines of goods, but doesn't have a camera department, or radio sales department, which could do well with the right attention. Or the store might have a line that is moving slowly.

If the store manager is offered either a monthly rent or a percentage of sales, it could be profitable for both parties. In the case where stores turn over sections to independent people on a percentage of sales basis, it is generally agreed that all transactions go through the store's cash register system. For example, I noticed in Waikiki that one of the world's largest and most beautiful Woolworth stores has a number of departments operated by women who are in business for themselves. Among those rented sections are gifts and souvenirs. The operators said they were doing very well. All sales go through Woolworth cash machines and the company rebates a percentage of sales to the tenant. Operators observe store hours, employ their own help, and buy their own goods.

Do Your Own Buying

Different types of stores have various methods of renting out partial premises. Some stores take care of cleaning, advertising, and insurance. Straight rentals may run from one hundred to five hundred dollars a month. On percentage of sales agreements, rental could depend on monthly gross. This might run from ten to twenty-five percent with a one to five percent escalation clause for higher sales. A basic rate might be twenty percent on annual sales of up to fifty thousand dollars, and a reduction to three percent on any gross sales over this.

A Florida drug store chain sub-contracts its camera department and radio sales section. All sales go through company cash registers. If a customer has picked up an item at another counter and happens to come to a sub-contractors counter, cash transactions are handled by the operator pressing a certain key indicating it was an "outside" sale.

The "independent" department has many benefits. An enthusiastic camera buff can build sales in a photo department to a much higher level than "just another" clerk.

Small stores sometimes have available space that can be turned into profitable departments. Starting capital can be low and the new "boss," who may prefer working busy weekends or nights, can engage a knowledgable person to handle things during slower periods.

30
Calligraphy is in Demand

A spare-time business that is becoming more popular is the art of calligraphy. This is also known as art lettering. Kits can be bought in stationery and art stores for under ten dollars, and the more expert person can add supplies as his or her skills demand more sophisticated instruments.

Special lettering is often required by companies giving gifts to retirees and for other special company events such as golf tournaments or competitions where certificates are distributed. This specialized lettering, which can be done in any size, is often in demand by family and friends or community services for gifts and presentations for special occasions. For instance, poets like to use special lettering when framing copies of their poems for gifts or for sale.

Ads in local weeklies are usually productive in finding markets for this kind of work.

31
Specialty Catering Comes Alive

In the past few years a relatively new type of business has blossomed. This is restaurant, party and office catering.

I know of one woman who bakes cakes for restaurants. She does the baking at home, and her son delivers to the customers. Some popular items are Black Forest cake, Danish pastry, and home-style cheese cake.

A few years ago, a cook in a restaurant might have been expected to make cakes as part of his duties. But today, there isn't always a need for a lot of specialty baking, and cooks sometimes don't have the time to do this kind of cooking. Also, pastry chefs are demanding higher and higher wages.

However, many small restaurants like to offer specialities, so when "home catering" arrived it fulfilled a demand.

Some home caterers deliver every second day, and charge a wholesale price of about eight dollars per pie. A restaurant might charge two dollars for a slice of cheese cake and will get approximately seven slices from one pie or cake.

One man offers a special home catering service. He advertises with house-to-house circulars. In his ad he offers to bake cakes for any occasion; weddings, birthdays, anniversaries, Christmas, pool parties in the summertime, etc. He guarantees to deliver on the date and approximate time required. He puts his phone number on the circulars and says he gets plenty of calls. He charges an average of fifteen dollars for a good size cake.

It is estimated that a quarter of North Americans eat out at least once a week, so catering specialties to smaller restaurants is a growing business.

32
Tutoring at Home

Teaching a subject at home is very popular. Depending upon your abilities, you might teach a language, reading skills, mathematics or arts and crafts.

One woman teaches fine art to young people and older students. She started teaching in her home but her courses became so popular that she rented a two-room apartment, and now works from there. She charges ten dollars for a two hour session, and limits the class to eight students. She occasionally runs classified ads in the local weekly to promote her business, when her class drops below a minimum.

33
Teaching Music

Music lessons have always been a popular cottage industry for those with the ability to teach and inspire students. For example, a woman teaches organ playing. She primarily explains the intricacies of organ playing, and the chords and a love for the instrument. She purchased a used organ for eight hundred dollars, although it required tuning. According to her, there has been such an upswing in the sale of these instruments that the demand for teachers is unprecedented.

34
The Sandwich Wagon

Many large office buildings have their own lunch services, and most factories are no doubt solicited by the professional food wagon services with trucks and uniformed attendants. However, there are countless small offices and private homes where a daily delivery of fresh sandwiches and sweet goods would be appreciated.

If you are interested in this business, your market is the small outlets where you might not have more than a dozen customers at any one call. You might take orders the previous day and leave a dozen lunch boxes, consisting of a sandwich, a cake or piece of pie, and some fruit. There are also shut-ins who would appreciate this service once or twice a week. A house-to-house circular mentioning your prices and items available would no doubt bring in business.

People working in small offices often appreciate such a service, particularly when the weather is bad. If you start your deliveries at ten in the morning and finish by 12:30 you can cover a lot of ground. A station wagon would be ideal for deliveries which would be made right to the door.

Some firms, who now have dozens of vehicles, started small.

35
Telephone Soliciting

Here's another angle to an old business that could be of interest to you.

A rug cleaning company was interested in soliciting sales by phone. A college professor, who had two days a week free agreed to be responsible for the work, but, instead of doing the phoning himself, he advertised for hired sales help. He then supplied telephones and working space to interested people, and offered them a guaranteed minimum wage, which he paid from the commission paid him by the rug cleaning company.

So, this operation works as follows. The phone solicitor, after making a sale, fills out a sheet giving the prospect's name and address. The rug cleaning firm then sends an estimator to give the customer the cost of the work and the time the job will be done. The customer agrees and signs the order. The workmen are paid when the job is finished. The rug company then pays the professor his commission, and he, in turn, pays his staff.

36
Salesman Becomes Furniture Finisher

A man of thirty-five made his living working as a salesman for a paper firm selling to printers. But his firm was sold to a competitor that already had a staff of salespeople, and this young man was let go. He had a wife and two children and little money in the bank. However, he did have an idea, and as it turned out, it was a good one.

He had a garage which, over the space of five years, he had turned into a workshop. His hobby was furniture. He refinished old tables, bureaus, etc. He rebuilt the damaged parts, and even made special furniture to order and to fit certain sections of the home. He had been doing work for relatives and friends, basically charging just for the materials he had to buy. Occasionally someone brought in an antique piece of furniture to have it repaired or refinished, and he often got a good price for this work.

He decided to try to make a living from his hobby. He loved the work and he had the equipment he needed, so the starting capital was almost nil. Besides he would save money working at home. He wouldn't have the cost of daily transportation to work, or lunches to buy, and as far as dressing up, a windbreaker and a pair of jeans would be fine.

He had an inexpensive circular printed by a nearby copy shop. The cost was fifteen dollars for five hundred copies. Then he got a neighbour's boy to drop the circulars in mailboxes within a half-dozen blocks. He kept a note of the area covered, so he wouldn't duplicate it when he distributed another.

Business Flows In

He was amazed at the results he got. It seemed that just about everyone had at least one piece of furniture that needed refinishing. For a year after this man started in business, he was making as much — or more — than he had made as a salesman. Now he is his own boss, works from home, and makes his own hours. If you possess this talent, and have the tools, you just might succeed at this as well.

37
Delivery Service

If you have a vehicle, you can offer a delivery service to businesses in your area. This can be a part-time service for a number of retail outlets. Many stores charge their customers for delivery and would welcome an independent service as it saves them the trouble and cost of operating their own. Many retailers who don't already have this service can be convinced that delivery will boost sales, as well as help shoppers who don't drive a car.

38
Service Needs

Services in demand include walking dogs regularly, checking on people's houses for them when they are on vacation or away on business, feeding and caring for pets while the family is away, as well as looking after the lawn and picking up the mail for absentee families.

39
Steak and Kidney Pies in Demand

A man with culinary experience has developed two cooking skills that are paying off handsomely. He cooks steak and kidney pies and apple pies, skills he learned when he was a cook in the navy. He has developed two main sources of sales. The first is neighbours and friends, who drop around on the days when these baked goods are available.

The second sales outlet is a nearby bake shop. They take as large a quantity as he has available. Usually it's steak and kidney pies on Saturdays, and apple pies on Tuesdays. His wholesale price is two dollars and fifty cents per pie, and the bakery charges four dollars.

This cook will also do a little special baking on request, such as pumpkin pies and birthday cakes. He will also prepare and cook turkeys and hams for buffets for the local bakery upon request.

40
Dried Flowers are Popular

If you have a sunny porch or a greenhouse, you might consider growing flowers all winter, as well as in summer, and drying them for sale.

Commercial houses will tell you which flowers look best when dried, and which are most suitable. You can then dry the flowers and sell them to stores that sell them year round. Also, many hardware, convenience, and especially gift stores find that dried flowers sell well.

Retailers might place the dried flowers around the base of fresh flowers, to increase their price. Dried flowers can be made into bouquets and sold separately to people who use them as table decorations. Also, the people who do this as a profitable hobby report that dried flowers give lasting enjoyment and are a very popular item.

41
Complete Catering Service

Two women started a home catering service that quickly grew, and, after a year, they rented a store where they were able to attract passing trade. The day they opened their store, they offered free coffee and sample slices of their cakes. The place was crowded and many orders developed. Eventually, they were able to expand their space, offer courses on making chocolates, chocolate novelties and baking. They also had counters offering special items for parties, with emphasis on paper goods, such as party streamers, paper plates and napkins.

One of their big attractions are courses in baking and decorating cakes for all occasions. They offer afternoon classes with a couple of grandmothers on hand to babysit the preschoolers, evening classes for working people, and even Saturday classes for those who cannot attend during the week. Also, they sell instruction books and all the equipment — molds, chocolate tablets in various colours, and the mixers and decorations necessary to suit any occasion.

Their catering terms require a deposit on an order to ensure the customer's return and to offset their upfront costs. Although they do not offer delivery, two-day service is offered. This store which caters quality food and good service is a boon to a busy neighbourhood.

42
Teaching English

A lot of people have emigrated to North America in the past few years, and the immigration rate is increasing all the time. Many of these people want their children to learn to speak English well, and to learn it as quickly as possible.

A qualified teacher I know, has not worked in a school for several years but has many students. She works from her home, and she has been tutoring some students on a one-hour a week basis for almost two years. She says that "almost all of the students are going to regular schools, or will be shortly, and take their instruction at hours convenient to them, often just one pupil at a time. The youngsters feel more comfortable in private sessions, and respond quickly."

Qualified teachers can demand high hourly rates. A classified ad usually brings good results.

43
I Love to Cook

A lot of people would be delighted to learn how to prepare foreign food, such as Chinese, Italian, and German dishes. A couple of women, knowledgable in these types of cooking, gave lessons. One week would be Italian, the next week Chinese, and the next week, German. Courses were offered in the middle of the day, and cost twelve dollars a lesson, which included a meal which the students prepared.

The most popular specialities include buffet meals, soufflés, and casseroles. In fact, anyone with knowledge of specialty cooking of almost any type could suggest starting a service of this kind. Run a few classified ads to gauge interest.

You can always brush up on your specialty by reading up on it at the library.

44
Repair Appliances

With the increasing cost of purchasing household items, such as toasters, irons, and other small home appliances, many people find it cheaper to get an appliance repaired rather than buy a new one.

If you have the ability to repair these appliances, call on hardware and other stores, pick up appliances that need repairs and give the stores a percentage of the price you charge.

One young man has a panel truck on the sides of which are painted various electrical appliances. He advertises and calls at private homes and picks up items to be repaired. He was once a bus driver and did this work only in his spare hours but the business became so profitable, he now devotes all his time to it.

45
Home Office Service

People with typewriters often make a good income by doing typing for professional people and small business. This work might be typing invoices, letters, or other business material.

The easiest way to get into this business is either by making personal calls, or by sending a photocopied letter with your phone number to prospects. A big market can be found by placing an ad on a college or university bulletin board. Busy people are always looking for help with typing. Also send your ad to local writers' clubs.

You could arrange to pick up the work or have it mailed. A steady customer could supply a considerable amount of this work to a "home" typist. Business people prefer this arrangement because they don't have to supply a working area, equipment, make salary deductions for the payment of taxes, medicare, holiday pay, etc.

Home typists are in business for themselves, and can work whenever they choose.

46
"We'll do Anything"

This idea started in Tokyo, and has proven successful in North America also. It's a great spare-time program, and there is a need for it. You don't have to be a professional *anything* to succeed.

Here are the kind of jobs to expect: someone is having trouble with a sticking window; another person needs a grocery order, but can't leave the house; a third person wants the dog walked every day; someone else wants the windows washed; a store needs someone for two hours a day to deliver orders. And so it goes on. You would be amazed how many calls can come in, and the kind of services that are required.

What About Prices?

For a senior citizen or a handicapped person, even the simplest home help services are appreciated — particularly in bad weather. It may not seem important to anyone else, but to the housebound customer it's *very* important. But be careful what you charge. If you over-charge you will lose not only this customer but other possible customers, as word of mouth can make or break a business of this kind.

If you set a two dollar minimum this will probably be satisfactory, particularly if you designate a specific amount of time for the job, and plan to make a lot of calls in the same area around the same time. You will find that some people call you regularly to do odd jobs.

47
Carpet Cleaning — Big Business

It might not sound glamourous but it sure can be profitable. Almost all homes have some carpets or rugs which have to be cleaned. Rugs should also be washed a couple of times a year. Supermarkets and other stores rent shampoo equipment (at eight dollars, or more, a day) to wash carpets and rugs, but, homemakers find them heavy to handle, and they require a large quantity of expensive cleaning fluids. Supermarkets do a considerable amount of business in rentals, but by the time a machine is rented and the necessary cleaning liquids bought, the whole procedure can be expensive and tiresome.

One entrepreneur, who is also a full-time teacher offers to wash carpets at a price dependent upon size. He bought a commercial cleaner for about seven hundred and fifty dollars. He leaves school at 3:00 p.m. and by 4:00 p.m. is on his first job. This could pay him as much as fifty dollars. He may even do another job before he quits for the evening, and, of course, he often works all day Saturday. He says he sometimes clears a thousand dollars a month.

People pass his name along, and this results in a lot of business. Then, of course, there are repeat sales. Some people who want to get into the business but don't want to buy a machine right way, rent a machine when they get a job. Sometimes a used heavy-duty unit can be picked up cheaply, as well as large quantities of soap at wholesale prices.

This is fairly heavy work but homemakers appreciate it. You bring the machine and soap to their home and there is no messy machine for them to clean and put away when the job is done. It is an idea worth investigating, and might become a lucrative full-time occupation.

48
Manuscript Typing

Most authors are poor typists and editors object to messy manuscripts. So, if you are a neat typist, have a typewriter that turns out professional-looking material, and you are also able to correct any grammatical errors, you might find this work interesting and profitable. A productive author can give you a lot of work. Moreover, if you get along with a writer or better still, a word processor, you could work for him or her for years. Two or three active writers can keep you busy.

The easiest way to attract customers is to run classified ads in writers' and teachers' magazines and various scholarly publications. A publication with a good book review section could also bring results.

49
The Research Business

Authors frequently require someone to do research work. One writer doing a book on ancient Spain had a research person working almost full time gathering data. Libraries, archives, etc. are an excellent source of material.

A woman writing a restaurant guide had a researcher checking out various spots for type of food, specialities, and prices. The information was usually gathered by writing or phoning restaurants for their menus, and then selecting two or three specialities for the book. A conscientious researcher can save an author many working hours, and time is money when freelancing.

50
Janitorial Services in Demand

Both stores and smaller office buildings require people to keep the premises clean. A new business that supplies this service on a contract basis will find that it is in great demand. Sometimes, tenants hire their own cleaner, and other times it is done by the building owner. For a larger building it may be the superintendant's job.

One way to organize such a firm is to appoint one manager for so many cleaning locations. Thus one manager may handle a half-dozen locations, while another manager may look after a small office building with a dozen tenants.

A man I know was offered the opportunity of taking over janitorial services for a small office building of twelve suites. The offices required cleaning three times a week, from six to nine in the evening. The pay was two hundred dollars a week. This man and his seventeen year old son did the work. Soon he was able to add three more buildings, and today has a staff of twenty-five cleaners. His company covers the city and the gross is in excess of two hundred thousand dollars a year.

Ads in the yellow pages are the best places to get business of this kind.

51
The "800" Phone Numbers and Credit Cards

Multi-millions of dollars' worth of business is done through the use of credit cards and the "800" toll free phone system. The seller with this set-up offers the buyer the opportunity of calling from hundreds of miles away, without any phone charges. The sales offer can be just about anything. Major firms use this sales method. Hotel rooms, magazine subscriptions, ads, real estate, specialty foods, and so on are sold this way. It is just as convenient for the purchaser as phoning a local store.

The rate the business pays for this helpful phone service depends on how wide a territory is required. The business office of the telephone company has this information.

Many firms advertise their free long-distance number in print and on the air, especially those that sell records and tapes, books, cosmetics, etc.

You may also be interested in becoming a merchant member of a credit card organization. This is a valuable service for those customers who wish to pay with credit cards whether or not you offer the long-distance system.

Becoming a Credit Card Merchant

First you would get what is known as a merchant's number. Check with your bank. There is a cost of around twenty-five dollars (sometimes a little lower or higher). There is a percentage of sales charge for these transactions. The percentage depends on the total transactions you put through. The larger the total, the smaller the fee. Charges of four to five percent are average. You are supplied with printed slips by the credit card people. You write in the name and address of your customer, his or her account number and expiry date of his or her card. The bank will credit the amount of the order to your account immediately. Being a credit card merchant increases sales, especially for out-of-town customers, who respond to your ads.

Purchases made in person by a customer require a credit card machine supplied by the credit card company. But for the telephone orders or for out-of-town customers, no machine is required, all entries can be processed by hand. Validity of a credit card can be established immediately by the credit card organization. You simply call them on the telephone, give them your merchant number, your customer's card number and expiry date and the amount of the transaction. They will then give you an authorization number which you also write on the slip. Being a credit card merchant is a good way to build out-of-town sales.

52
Holding Seminars

Do you like to talk? Lecture? Give advice? Have you a specialty? Are you particularly knowledgable on a subject? If you can answer "yes" to most of these questions, holding a series of seminars might be a great spare-time money-making idea for you.

Lectures can be on almost any topic. You have heard them on travel, writing, history, cottage industries, health, wealth, etc.

Today, people seem to have two main ambitions; to get new information, and to make extra money. It's a national craze, and you might be able to do a lot of people a lot of good, and cash in on it, too!

Three Ways to Cash In

You have to be paid for your work, and there are three main ways to go about it. You can rent a hall (often a hotel room) for about forty dollars and charge each guest a fee. You might hold three sessions, a week apart, and charge five to ten dollars a meeting. Or you might have someone sell "further information" booklets after your talk. Or you might offer a course (that would really be a series of pamphlets).

There must be an element of excitement in your offer and advertising. There is no place here for the introvert. You will have to appear dynamic and confident.

I was once invited to speak at a large library, and when the meeting started at 8:00 p.m. there was an audience of five. I went ahead with my talk, as I was getting two hundred and fifty dollars anyway, but later I checked with the library. I discovered that the person in charge of advertising special events, had placed only one classified ad, and that no news release had been sent to the press or radio stations.

Two weeks later I spoke at another gathering at a Holiday Inn. The large room was crowded and it was an enjoyable evening. Advertising and PR had brought in both members and friends. So make sure your seminars get publicity. This is most important.

53
Land for Quick Cash Crops

Another case study will best illustrate this. A man owned some unused farm land. An entrepreneur approached this man and offered to pay him two hundred and fifty dollars for the use of five acres for a year. The owner agreed as the money would be helpful at tax time. Then the entrepreneur arranged to have the sod on the acres of land turned over and strawberry plants planted.

As soon as the berries began to ripen, he placed classified ads giving readers information on his berries and details about when they could come and pick them. He says people flocked to the farm and picked their own berries. All containers were weighed, and the cash was collected. He had a good season and said he intends to rent more space and add tomatoes.

54
Selling Used Vacuum Cleaners Brings Extra Cash

There is always a demand for used vacuum cleaners providing they are in working condition. One lady is making excellent money in her spare time as a result of this experience.

She had purchased a new vacuum cleaner, and being enterprising she placed a two dollar classified ad in her local weekly. The old machine was working and she asked seventy-five dollars for it, and had at least a dozen calls. It sold immediately.

Her children were grown up, and she had plenty of spare time, so she decided to cash in on this little experience.

Her new machine was bought from a salesman who had come to the house. So she phoned and asked him if he ever had any old machines. He said he seldom mentioned that when trying to sell a new one, as many customers wanted him to take their old machine as a trade-in. In fact, he said he had a half-dozen in his garage right now that the woman could have for twenty-five dollars each.

She bought them and got a young man who was interested in mechanics to look them over. In no time they were buzzing merrily and this woman put a classified ad in the newspaper. The ad read as follows: Vacuum, good make, in working condition. Phone ****

The paper came out, and once again she began getting phone calls. She had placed a piece of rug in her basement so the customer could try out the cleaner. She asked fifty to seventy-five dollars and was able to dispose of most of them. Then, by calling on vacuum cleaner stores, she was often able to make additional arrangements to buy used vacuums.

She has been doing this for almost three years, and is quite successful at it. If she wants to take a holiday, she just doesn't advertise during that period. She also stops during mid-summer and major holidays.

55
New Roads — New Opportunities

The openings of new highways to areas which formerly had only country roads offer new sales territories for many people.

A man working in Toronto had purchased two acres of land with a farmhouse fronting on a quiet country road. His land was about sixty-five miles from Toronto. A highway was constructed over the old road and traffic had increased. Instead of being annoyed by the noise he had a 12 x 12 foot structure built at the corner of his entrance lane and the main road leaving space for parking and he opened his roadside store.

He kept his job and opened only on weekends. He stocked locally produced maple syrup, bread, fruit, vegetables, and other produce. He claims he makes more here than at his regular job. His season is mid-April to the end of October. He says there is always something to sell — even jams, pickles, and knitted goods.

Anyone interested in something like this might find it worthwhile to drive out to country areas and look around.

Some Business Facts

Knowing how business operates in general is always useful, and often helps in making important decisions.

Should You Incorporate?

Incorporating your company provides some advantages in taxes, expenses and in limiting personal liability. First, get the advice of your lawyer and your accountant. As your accountant will explain, you will have to have a CA (chartered accountant) prepare annual financial statements and do your corporate income tax returns.

You will have to decide dates for your company's financial year (any twelve month period), as changing this date later on, is not easy.

If you incorporate your business can be called a corporation, incorporated, or limited. It's a matter of choice; the cost is the same. The cost varies from a couple of hundred dollars to five hundred dollars, plus your legal fees. Incorporated companies require company directors, a president, who is usually the owner, at least in the case of small companies, a secretary/treasurer, and a vice-president is desirable.

The Value of Being Incorporated

It is said that incorporation gives your operation credibility and substantiality in the minds of the people with whom you deal. But this is not always the case with experienced business people. They know from experience that cheques from limited companies can bounce as easily as those from individuals.

On Getting a Loan

If, as president of a limited company, you go under, only the assets of your company can be seized. The only exception is when you have signed for anything personally. If you get a loan from a bank, you will have to guarantee this personally, unless the firm has excellent collateral. This means that, if you go under, the bank can take your home or other personal assets to cover any outstanding loan.

If you are forced into bankruptcy, in all likelihood it will be the bank that forces this action. If you are in a weak financial position, the bank is well aware of it. They'll be watching your overdraft, loan situation, cash flow, and so forth. Many business people who get into a weak position sell off as much as they can. This gives them some personal security before the axe falls. That is why people who are going to be forced under are not usually warned beforehand, so that those instituting the bankruptcy will have something to seize.

If you are signing personally for company loans, when declaring your personal assets make sure that you do own them. Mention any other loans you have outstanding and have made this same guarantee for.

Always read the small print in a loan application and guarantee form. If you do get a loan from the bank (rent their money — as they say in the trade), be aware of what your rights are and what the bank's rights are. For example, if your spouse owns most of your personal or company assets, this can cut down your borrowing power. A loan is a great servant, but a horrible master.

Discounting Your Invoices

There are firms who will advance money to you on the basis of signing over your receivables to them; in other words, this is the money you are owed for goods you sold. Say you invoiced ten thousand dollars in sales for the month concerned, but your payment terms are net thirty days. You find yourself in a cash flow bind and you need cash immediately. The cash advance on this ten thousand dollar figure might be in the vicinity of eight thousand dollars.

These "discounts" vary from area to area. Check closely before signing up. Short-term benefits from this practice include fast cash and no risk of bad debt on those invoices concerned. But if this is practiced regularly, it can remove all the profit from your business, especially if your net profit is something like ten percent (which is usual) and you're paying fifteen percent or more to a discount house.

Loan Firms Can be Helpful

A retired man in Florida was formerly the manager of the branch of a large loan company. He told me his firm had two main divisions. One was dedicated to lending large sums of money and the other to soliciting investors for their company. This latter division contacted people they knew had money and followed up enquiries from advertisments, with a view to getting more money into their company. Investment in their company was attractive because of the high interest rates it paid, and the solidity of their firm.

The company was always seeking people with good track records. People who were known to be able to turn loans into big money. This, of course, was how the company made its money. If they paid an interest on investments of ten percent, for example, and loaned the money at fifteen percent, they would gross five percent, and with millions of dollars coming and going, the profits were high.

The "Poor" Man Who Wanted a Loan

This retired manager said, "Sometimes I could see that a prospective borrower didn't have much in the way of assets, but there was a drive, a zest for doing things that I couldn't ignore. Even in our business you have to gamble sometimes."

"One day, a shabbily-dressed man came to my office for a loan. I looked out of my window and saw the ten-year-old car this fellow was driving. He said he lived in a small town and owned a bus company. He admitted he had only three buses, one of which he drove, and that he got them from a big city bus firm which had "retired" them. Their total value was a debatable five thousand dollars. He added that things were so bad that he gave his drivers free bus tickets, which they could sell in lieu of salary until things got better. However, he discovered the drivers were selling the tickets at various reduced prices in order to make money. However, it seemed that, within a year, a paper firm was going to use his bus line to take people to work."

My New Friend Makes a Loan

This potential borrower said he needed money right away — fifty thousand dollars; but he did not have the contract yet. He wanted the money to make a down payment on new buses, a garage and to hire staff.

"We gave him the money, " said the former loan officer, "and he left excitedly. He made his payments on time, and came back a year later for a half-million dollar loan for another business he wanted to buy. I noticed that his cash flow had increased remarkably in his bus company. This time he was driving a new car."

"Another year passed and this time he needed two million dollars to buy a big city bus line. I noticed he now had a Cadillac parked outside our office with a chauffeur waiting attentively."

"That was twenty years ago, and this man came to us any time he needed money. He did well with us, and we did well with him. I'm sure glad I took a chance on that poor fellow. Now he is a millionaire."

How Much Capital Do You Need?

Raising money to start a business isn't generally easy. I've known as many people who had big money and failed, as those who had little starting capital.

One person had adequate capital, rented an office, and decided to rent his furniture, and whatever else he thought he might need in the way of copying machines, typewriters, filing cabinets, desks, lighting, and so on. It was all top quality, and his monthly rental bill was about one thousand dollars. Next he hired expensive people, luring them from other companies.

At this point he had no ongoing business; just an idea. After six months, and having spent two hundred thousand dollars, he closed the doors. Yet if he had bought a few used pieces of furniture, rented a small office and done most of the work himself, testing as he went, it could have been a different story.

Accountants advise new businesses to start in small premises, and don't move until you are busting at the seams. Keep all costs down, such as phone, printing, and other daily items. Have your work done outside, rather than buying equipment and hiring expensive help.

Don't be too proud when you start a business. One man opened a small hardware store and, at night, called at nearby homes asking if the occupants had any windows that needed new glass. If they did, he took the window, repaired it next day, and delivered it that night. Before selling out he had built his little business into a chain of stores.

What About a Partnership?

A partnership depends mainly on the partners' personalities. A three-way partnership is better than a two-person partnership because, if you have a problem, you can always take a vote.

With a twosome, problems arise if one person has a stronger personality than the other. It often happens in two- and three-people partnerships that one person makes all the important decisions. It can be very embarrassing if one partner makes commitments, to which the other partner(s) objects. There have been stories where one partner has made a purchase, and the other partner demanded that the buyer pay for the item personally. In financial matters partners are equally liable.

Be Careful Taking Over Leases

Some shopping centres and individual stores have leases with subclauses that state that, if a place is sublet, the rent is automatically increased by a certain percent.

Rent must be judged by the annual business done or expected to be done. A thousand-dollars-a-month rent would be ridiculous for a business that was only doing, or expected to do, twenty-five thousand dollars of business a year.

Businesses for Sale

Proceed carefully when considering the acquisition of an existing business. It may happen that the owner of a business wants to sell because he has a long lease at a high rent which he has difficulty meeting. If buying, check on the value of any fixtures. They can probably be purchased at cheaper prices.

Renting Space

The amount you pay in rent should reflect the nature of your business. Sometimes a rent will be all right for one business, but completely out of line for another. For instance, a retailer selling big ticket items might find a two-thousand-dollar-a-month rent a good idea if the store sells five-hundred-and-fifty-dollar TV sets. But if the product is second-hand paperbacks, a high rent is not advisable. It is wise to check not only annual sales if buying an existing business, but also its profit if it is located in a shopping centre that takes an additional percentage of profits. Some businesses gross forty percent profit on a sale of one item, while others sell low-profit items and depend on high volume.

If you are going into a shopping mall, make sure of the restrictions in your lease. You may have to restrict sales to one type of merchandise, as another store may have sole rights to sell something you intended to add later.

For example, a gift shop owner was all excited about a line of novelty watches that she bought for the big sales season just ahead. When the novelty watches went on display, the store owner was advised that a jewellery store in the mall held the exclusive right to sell all types of watches and clocks.

Buying a Business?

Many businesses are offered for sale at a figure equal to the annual business done. A store owner doing one hundred thousand dollars a year may try to sell his business for one hundred thousand. If the annual gross profit was fifty thousand, then twice this profit might be a good buying price. If the annual net profit was nil, after the owner took out say twenty-five thousand dollars in salary then the asking price of one hundred thousand dollars would be far too high.

One general guideline is that sellers tend to ask four to five times their annual profit, after deducting a fair salary.

On a one-hundred-thousand-dollar investment, a person could take ten thousand dollars in straight interest without working. So this kind of investment, even on a time basis, should pay considerably more than ten percent, plus the operator's salary.

Don't Bite Off More Than You Can Chew

A man of thirty-two had a business opportunity. It looked good. He would have to stock large quantities of merchandise, but there was one steady customer who would more than keep the new business going. But the young man would need ten thousand dollars to start up. He had little money, so went to his father and got a loan.

Everything went well for six months. Then a competitor moved in with lower prices, and took the young man's major customer. He was in dire straights and soon was forced to close. The father lost his money.

The moral is "start in a small way and don't invest more than you can afford to lose if things don't turn out as you expected." Run tests, surveys; experiment. No matter what happens the experience can be priceless. Don't depend on only one or two accounts.

Almost all businesses today, no matter how large, were started by people with an idea, and usually little capital.

Setting Up Your Office

It is always a good idea to set up an office, even when operating from home. One of the essential requirements is a typewriter for producing invoices. What many small operators do to save money is type out a master invoice with your name, address, etc, and a letterhead. In the event that you want to use larger type for your name, go to an art or stationery store and get a package of stick-on type. When you have your invoice ready take it to a copy centre which will run off a couple of hundred of each of your items cheaply. You won't need a large quantity in case you want to make changes later.

You'll also need a few file folders which cost about fifteen cents each. You won't need a file cabinet yet. A cardboard box will be adequate. You will need a couple of inexpensive record books. The soft cover ones will do nicely.

In one book record your expenses, and in the other your sales. It is not necessary to record small purchases, such as a bottle of glue, unless it costs two or three dollars. Even then, you are wiser to enter a total of "petty cash" expenses in larger totals at the end of the week. It is best to have a large envelope in which you can deposit all the receipts you pick up, from travel expenses to stationery. For larger expenses, such as merchandise, printing, etc., pay by cheque. Keep the cheques when you get them back from the bank, as they will be your receipts.

An ongoing record quickly tells you if you are making money and where you are going. Good clear records are good business, but don't spend too much time on them. There's no profit here!

Keep Office Expenses Down

No matter what kind of business you are in, office expenses could sink you. When I started publishing my first magazine, I hired a bookkeeper. After six months she said she had to have an assistant. Six months later the assistant figured she could do a better job with an assistant of her own.

In the meantime, the editor decided an assistant editor would be nice, and the advertising manager didn't know how he could make all the necessary calls without help. By this time I had taken on an office manager to look after everyone, although our business hadn't shown much of an increase in income from the beginning. In fact, now I was losing real money. We had large payroll expenses, insurance costs, travel expenses, additional space, and other costs — most of which were created purely by staff necessity.

One day my accountant discussed the problem at length. "Cut your staff to one, " he said.

"But I have fourteen people here. How can I manage?"

"Simple," he argued. "Do what an increasing number of small and medium size firms are doing. Let the people who work for you, work for themselves."

I guess I looked puzzled. My accountant laid out a plan for me. I arranged to have salesmen work for themselves on a straight commission of twenty-five percent. Editors worked for themselves at so much an issue. This worked out even better as I added more magazines.

There were other jobs which I handled the same way. Sometimes people worked part-time in the office, sometimes at home. This way staff was dramatically reduced to one key office person who kept things hopping.

In the event that people are working on commission, check with your accountant to find out the maximum amount a company can pay employees per week in your area, before it has to start making deductions.

Ways of Cutting Starting Costs

Very often, wholesalers will extend very favourable credit terms to new businesses. Wholesalers are always looking for new accounts, so have a chat with them and tell them what you want.

Also, a landlord with a store that has been empty for a while may give you a reduction in rent for the first year.

The two biggest expenses in starting a business (besides stock) are salaries and rent (if you need outside quarters). Run a check and see how much pedestrian traffic passes by a location you are considering renting for a store. If it is largely car traffic you expect to get, check on parking. People might be interested in visiting you but they aren't going to spend a lot of time looking for a place to park.

How much capital you need to start will depend on the business you choose and its location. It is better to spend more for rent and get a busy spot, then to spend little and have to spend a great deal in advertising to draw people into your place of business.

Get Out if Losses Mount

If you are in a business that is losing money and you see no solution, cut the umbilical cord and get out. It may be your baby, and you love it, but if it is continuing to cost you money then the sensible thing to do is get out before these losses pull you overboard. It's better to get out and cut your losses.

If you have a lease, go to your landlord. Tell him frankly how badly things are going and that if you stay on you will owe him more rent then you do now and that he will have a tough — if not impossible — job to collect. If he lets you out maybe he can rent again quickly. If this is impossible, make a deal. Tell him you'll pay two or three month's rent over a period of time.

Remember, you should study your business venture in advance. Know what you are doing. Don't play in shark infested waters if you are a baby minnow. You could be eaten alive.

Becoming an "Instant" Millionaire

Turn on the radio, especially between midnight and five in the morning, or check magazines and newspapers, and you'll find all sorts of tips on how to get rich quick. It would seem that all one has to do is pay your money, follow the easy directions, and in no time you will be wealthy.

I've studied case histories of many successful people and their formula is usually "start with a good idea and a lot of hard work." A lot of people will help you if you ask them, but *you're* the one who will have to carry the ball.

You may not always succeed in your first effort or two, but, whether you realize it or not, you will be getting closer to your goal. You'll be working on the the law of averages.

A salesman reported that his income came from one sale in every ten calls. He didn't worry if he made a lot of calls without success because he figured that, according to the law of averages, he'd succeed with one call in ten.

Success Ratio

A report shows that twenty-five percent of the population are fighting desperately to keep financially stable. These are people who seldom pay their bills on time, have poor credit ratings, and constantly live from hand-to-mouth.

It is estimated that fifty percent of the population are also in a tight squeeze. However, by careful watching, and often by holding down two jobs, they are able to keep afloat. But it is not always easy. This group is always hoping for better things, and greater opportunities for their offspring.

Then there is the third group. This twenty-five percent seem to do all right. We all know people in this bracket. They own good homes, drive expensive cars, hold professional positions, or operate profitable businesses, take luxurious holidays, and seldom seem to have any money problems. No one knows what main factor has contributed in these people's success. Is it education? Hard work? Personality? A fast mind? Luck? Maybe it's a little of each.

Your Competition

Your competition in life and business is this last twenty-five percent of the population. The other two groups are so busy with their own problems they don't even know you exist.

But the latter group are always aware of what's happening. Unless you're on your toes they could "buy you at one corner and sell you at the next," before you could figure out what was happening.

Today, success means keeping up with things. Population has increased and education has improved over the past few years. Communications media provide instant information and it is aimed at you. Be aware of what's going on; observe, set your own course and plough ahead. There are all kinds of opportunities out there waiting for you to take advantage of.

Go Public?

Many small business people have wondered whether they should go public — i.e. convert a portion of their company's value into shares which would be sold on the stock market. Such an operation is known as "going public," with a report on business, profits, etc., open to any interested party. A non-public firm has no stock on the market, therefore information about the company is not available to the public.

To go public you have to be doing a substantial amount of business. You may want to sell shares to enlarge or expand your company. Some people have been able to buy two or three small firms and bring them into their existing company to give their operation a more solid footing.

A stockbrokage firm usually has what is known as an "underwriting division."

A stockbroker has a position of trust, so he will usually deal only in the stocks that his company feels they can recommend. Prior to taking your firm public, many procedures are required. Lawyers and accountants will be called in to prepare various documents and financial reports. These papers will be examined by government security commissions to check on the company and number of shares being offered. These various costs of preparing and offering can be substantial.

All sorts of things happen when a stock hits the street. It may go out at twenty dollars a share and jump to triple this figure, or higher, in a short time. This sometimes happens when a long-established private (family-owned) company goes on the market. It may jump so high that shares are split. For instance, a one hundred dollar share might be replaced by four twenty-five dollar shares. This is a very common practice that makes cheaper shares available to more people.

Other stock offerings may barely move when they hit the market, or occasionally they may depreciate. World affairs and markets can affect stock prices. Anything can happen!

It Pays to Listen

Many business people say it pays to listen rather than talk. There are countless examples of people who have made fortunes from a stray remark they heard.

It is reported that John Jacob Astor, later to become a fur trader and wealthy merchant, was a passenger on a boat full of immigrants bound for New York from Europe. He had no money, but believed the new world would be good to him. He came up from his steerage quarters to get a breath of fresh air as the ship neared New York. He was standing near two men, when one said, "I understand they are bringing in all kinds of furs around Quebec City. If someone bought a few and brought them to the States they could make big money."

Astor thought about this for a long time and eventually made his way to where trappers were bringing in their pelts. He succeeded in making a fortune.

Another example is that of a Torontonian who said he overheard a chance remark that a certain secondary street would be important when a new city subway station was built near it. He bought two run-down houses on the street immediately, and did extremely well when the subway line eventually opened. He had replaced the two old houses with a large apartment block.

Can You Protect Your Idea?

So you have a great idea! What will you do with it? Protect it! You can patent it or if it is something written, you can copyright it. However, with regard to copyright, only the entire written work can be copyrighted; ideas alone are not protected.

Of course you can trademark your product's name and design, which could be important. This can be done through a patent lawyer but it is a costly procedure.

If you want to copyright anything, contact: In Canada, Consumer and Corporate Affairs, Copyright Office, Place du Portage, Phase 1, 50 Victoria Street, Ottawa-Hull, Ontario, K1A 0C9.

In the United States write to the Register of Copyrights, Library of Congress, Washington, D.C., 20559, U.S.A.

Our Customer

In business honesty is the best policy. Small stores have become big business because of their policies. The Eaton department store chain built their business on the slogan, "Goods Satisfactory or Money Refunded."

At one point Timothy Eaton's first store was on the east side of Toronto's Yonge Street. He decided it was time for a move. He discussed the move with his wife and she said, quoting the slogan of the day, "Go West, young man." So he moved across the street from where he built an empire.

Thirteen Steps to Success

Many business people have failed because of some simple thing they did or didn't do. Before you make what could be an important business decision, although you might not realize it's importance at the time, discuss the idea with others . . . experts if possible.

1
Adequate Insurance

Insurance, including a regular updated replacement value estimate, is very important. This applies to buildings *and* their contents. Inadequate insurance has been the underlying cause of many a bankruptcy. Contact your local insurance broker for full details about your business.

2
Getting a Loan

If you get a loan from a bank or other source, be aware if you personally (as well as your company) are responsible. If your company goes under, the people who rented you the money will insist on full payment. They could seize your personal assets, such as your car or house.

3
Check that Lease

If you are taking over a sublet, particularly from a shopping centre, check all the clauses. Is there a percentage charge on annual business, as well as rent? Is a new tenant expected to pay a higher rent than the old tenant? When the lease expires, can you renew without an increase?

4
Know Your Customer

If you get a large order from a new or even a repeat customer, it is worth checking their credit rating. Even if it is an old established firm, their financial situation may have changed. Or perhaps the company was sold and the new owner is not as solid as the previous one. Your bank can sometimes check for you.

5
Watch Over-Buying

You may be offered a special price on merchandise if you place a large order. Then you find that you've tied up your capital by over-ordering and you are stuck with slow-moving inventory. Lower unit costs don't always translate into bigger profits.

6
Do a Survey

Before starting a business it pays to find out if there is a need for what you intend to offer. Talk to suppliers, and possible customers. You will pick up valuable information.

7
Know Your Product

If you're in business, become an authority on your product or service matter pertaining to it. Study up on it. Learn as much as you can about it. Knowledge plus enthusiasm is a wonderful combination.

8
Know Your Competition

Know who they are and what they're doing. If they have been around a long time, they must be doing something right. Do not underestimate them.

9
Advertising?

Start small. Offer low prices and back it up with quality and service. This will bring customers in and keep them. A good bet these days is radio. Cheaper advertising costs are available from midnight to five in the morning on most radio stations. Ask your radio station advertising rep to tell you what they can do for you.

10
Become a Credit Card Merchant Member

It costs only a few dollars to join, plus a small percentage of your total credit card sales. In addition, accepted credit cards provides a convenience for many shoppers.

11
Maintain Proper Business Records

Not only are these necessary for tax filing purposes, but they will give you an instant picture of what your costs are, your profits, and help you to plan where you are going. A good accountant is invaluable. Before hiring a lawyer or accountant ask what their charges are.

12
Hire Honest and Reliable Staff

An employee is a representative of your company and should reflect the policies that you put in place. Train them well, check on them regularly. Remember, a dishonest employee can clean you out in no time. This is something most stores watch for, and often they insure people handling cash.

13
Practise Good Working Habits

At the beginning of your business venture, you will no doubt start early and work late. One wealthy man has said that his formula for success was simple, "Early to bed and early to rise, work like hell and advertise." Yes advertising is important, but so are good working habits.

If you eventually have a staff, they will probably follow the boss's lead. So do what you want your staff to do, set an example. Be punctual, work hard, and don't take lengthy lunch breaks too often, or frequent holidays . . . or you may come to work one day and ask, "What happened to the business?"

Notes

Notes